ENHANCING YOUR JOURNEY

A Biblical Guide To A More Powerful Prayer Life

MARLA A. MCCARTHY

RLF
Real Life Series Publishing

For permissions, inquiries, or bulk orders, please contact:
rlspublishing@gmail.com

Published by
The Real Life Series Publishing Co., LLC
All rights reserved.
Printed in the United States of America
www.thereallifeseries.com

First Edition: June 2025
ISBN: 979-8-9989754-3-1
Library of Congress Control Number: 2025911447

Scripture Acknowledgments:

Scripture quotations marked (KJV) are taken from the King James Version of the Bible. All scripture quotations in this book, except those noted otherwise, are taken from the King James Version of the Bible.

Scripture quotations marked (NKJV) are taken from the New King James Version®. Copyright © 1982 by Thomas Nelson. Used by permission. All rights reserved.

Publisher Contact:
The Real Life Series Publishing Co., LLC
Email: rlspublishing@gmail.com

DEDICATION

This book is dedicated to the memory of my late beloved mother, Deborah Hollins.

Your life was a testament to the power of faith, the beauty of unconditional love, and strength found in prayer. Through your words and actions, you showed me that a heart grounded in prayer can weather any storm and find peace in every season.

As a devoted wife, a nurturing mother, and a pillar in our church and community, you lived each day with grace, compassion, and unwavering faith. Your kindness touched the hearts of all who knew you, and your love continues to echo through the lives of your children, grandchildren, great-grandchildren, and family.

You led by example, kneeling in prayer when times were tough, lifting others with words of encouragement, and praising God through every trial and triumph.

This book is dedicated to you, my first teacher in faith, whose love and prayers have shaped the foundation of my relationship with God. Your legacy of faithfulness, selflessness, and love will forever inspire me, and I pray that each page of this book reflects the lessons you so lovingly instilled in me.

This is another part of your legacy, Mommy. It's proof that a praying mother's influence echoes through generations.

With all my love and eternal gratitude,
— *Marla*

TABLE OF CONTENTS

Why You Need This Book

If there's one thing I've learned as a wife and mother of six sons and one daughter, it's that life is beautifully chaotic, full of joy, surprises, and moments that stretch me in ways I never expected. Between the endless laundry, cooking meals that seem to disappear before they even hit the table, unplanned catastrophes, and keeping up with the whirlwind of schedules, I've come to treasure one thing above all else: prayer.

In all honesty, prayer can sometimes feel like a mystery. We know we should pray, but are we doing it right? Is there a secret formula to getting God's attention? Does He have a heavenly spam filter blocking our requests? (Spoiler: No, but wouldn't that be something?)

This book serves as your roadmap to unlocking the power of prayer, the kind that moves mountains, transforms hearts, and brings about real change. If you've ever felt like your prayers are bouncing off the ceiling, if you've ever whispered a prayer and wondered if God was really listening, or if you've ever longed for deeper faith but didn't know where to start, you're in the right place. Together, we'll explore what Scripture teaches about prayer, how to grow your connection with God, and how to experience supernatural breakthroughs in your life.

As a mom, I've experienced countless moments when I've had no choice but to pray, whether it was for wisdom in handling a tough parenting situation, for peace when the house was full of noise and chaos, or for the strength to make it through a day when I felt I had nothing left to give. And you know what? God answered. Every single time. Not always in the way I expected, but always in the way *I needed*. If the answer is "no", I've been on this journey long enough to know that it means God is protecting me or He has something better in store. I can trust and relax in that, and I want that for you, too.

Prayer: The Key to a Transformed Life

Prayer isn't just a routine or an obligation; it's a lifeline. It's our opportunity to turn away from the worries of this world and focus on the One who holds it all together. It's a sacred moment to surrender our burdens and show our dependence on God. It's an open invitation to deepen our relationship with the One who loves us beyond measure.

Prayer isn't just about asking for things; it's about praise, gratitude, faith, worship, confession, and adoration. It's about shifting our mindset from "What if?" to "God will."

And here's the best part: ***prayer based on God's Word and promises changes things.***

- Prayer shakes things up in the world. (Acts 4:31)
- Prayer opens doors. (Acts 16:25-26)
- Prayer causes God to move. (1 Samuel 1:10–20, 1 Kings 18:41–45, 1 Chronicles 4:10, 2 Kings 20:1–6, 2 Chronicles 20:1–30, Daniel 9:1–23, Acts 4:23–31, Acts 12:5–11, Luke 22:39–46, Acts 10:1–4)

Prayer results in enlarged territory, protection from harm, deliverance from trouble, open doors, provision, and healing. It nourishes our souls daily (Matthew 6:11), sanctifies our minds, bodies, and spirits (1 Thessalonians 5:23), and reminds us of the power and authority we have in Jesus' Name (Luke 4:36, Luke 9:1, Luke 10:19, Acts 3:16).

The world, and even the busyness of our everyday lives, may try to convince you that prayer is a last resort. But the truth is, prayer is your first line of defense. It's how we fight our battles, find peace in the storm, and witness miracles unfold.

Whether you're new to prayer or have been praying for years, I invite you to join me on this journey. I promise you this: if you commit to deepening your prayer life, you will see and feel God move in ways you never imagined.

Are you ready? Because your prayer life is about to level up!

How This Book Complements the 'Enhancing Your Journey: 90-Day Prayer Journal

If you've picked up this book, chances are you're looking for more than just a theoretical understanding of prayer. You want real, practical steps to enhance your prayer life. That's where the *Enhancing Your Journey: 90-Day Prayer Journal* comes in.

This book is your guide, laying out biblical insights, scriptural foundations, and practical strategies to help you pray with power. The companion journal is your personal space to apply the knowledge you gain here. Together, they work hand in hand to transform your prayer life.

By using both, you will:

1. Develop consistency in prayer: The journal provides structured prompts to keep you engaged daily.
2. Track answered prayers: Seeing God's faithfulness in action strengthens your faith.
3. Deepen your relationship with God: Writing down reflections and spiritual insights helps you connect with God on a more intimate level.
4. Cultivate gratitude and worship: The journal encourages you to focus on wisdom, guidance, and thanksgiving as you record your prayers and God's responses.

Think of this book as the "how," and the journal as the "practice." Together, they will help you build a prayer life that is rich, fulfilling, and life-changing.

Friend, I know what it's like to feel worn down. I know what it's like to wonder if your prayers are making a difference. But I also know what it's like to watch God show up in big ways, quiet whispers, and miraculous turnarounds.

You don't have to figure it all out before you start. You just have to begin. And that's what this book invites you to do. Are you ready to move from overwhelmed to empowered? From confused to confident? From distracted prayers to destiny-shaping declarations?

Then let's begin. Because prayer is not just something we do; it's who we are. And sis, it's time to rise in prayer like never before. So grab your journal, open your heart, and let's take this journey together because your best prayer life starts now!

Quick Reference Guide to Life-Changing Prayer

The P.O.W.E.R. Prayer System ™: How to Use This Quick Reference Guide for Powerful, Focused Prayer

Sweet sister, I want to take a moment and wrap my arms around you through these pages and say this: you are not alone. Whether you're flipping through this book during your quiet time, stealing five minutes between carpool pickups, or reaching for it during a late-night moment of overwhelm, I created this section with you in mind.

This *Quick Reference Guide* is here to serve as your prayer lifeline: a practical, spirit-filled tool you can turn to when you don't know what to say, when your heart feels heavy, or when you need to go deeper but feel stretched thin. Think of it as your spiritual first aid kit that you can flip to quickly: simple, powerful, and ready when you need it most.

Each focused prayer tip is designed to help you zero in on specific areas of life where we all need God to move, areas like peace, healing, provision, direction, forgiveness, and strength. You'll find key Scriptures to pray, declarations to speak, and heart-centered prompts to guide you into deeper intimacy with the Father.

Here's how to use this section:

- Feel overwhelmed? Turn here first. Let these guided prayer starters ground you before you dive into the rest of the book.
- Feel stuck? Use the prayer points as a jumpstart. They're not meant to replace your words, but to stir them up.
- Need a breakthrough? Focus your prayers like a laser with the truth of God's Word. Scripture-backed prayer is your most potent weapon.
- Journaling through the 90-Day Journal? Pair your daily entries with the prayers in this section. Let it breathe fresh life into your

conversations with God.

These prayers tips and prompts aren't just nice words; they're battle-tested, Spirit-led, and full of power. They come from my own journey of crying out to God as a mother, wife, woman, and daughter of the King. I've whispered some of these prayers through tears. I've shouted others in joy. I've clung to these Scriptures in both storms and sunshine. And now, I'm placing them in your hands with love and expectation.

So take a breath. Open your heart. Let these words lead you back to the Source. And remember, your prayers are powerful, your voice matters, and heaven listens when you speak. Let's pray with boldness. Let's believe with childlike faith. Let's expect God to move. Because He will.

REMEMBER: PRAYER IS POWER

P - PRAISE positions your heart
O - ORDER focuses your mind
W - WORD strengthens your faith
E - EXPECT activates God's power
R - REPEAT builds lasting change

P - PRAISE & PREPARE

Start Every Prayer Session Right...
1. PRAISE GOD FOR WHO HE IS:
- "God, You are my Provider, Protector, and Peace"
- "Father, You are faithful, loving, and all-powerful."
- "Jesus, You are my Savior, Friend, and King"

2. PREPARE YOUR HEART:
- Quiet your mind and focus on God's presence
- Confess any sin or worry that's blocking your connection
- Declare your faith: "I believe You hear me and will answer."

3. QUICK PRAISE STARTERS:
- "Thank You, God, for..."
- "I worship You because You are..."
- "I'm grateful for how You..."

O - ORDER YOUR PRAYERS

Pray with Purpose and Structure...

1. THE DAILY PRAYER ORDER:

- Personal Needs - Your health, peace, wisdom, strength
- Family Focus - Spouse, children, extended family
- Others' Needs - Friends, community, world
- Future Vision - Dreams, goals, calling, legacy

2. SCRIPTURE-BASED ORDERING:

- Morning: Strength and wisdom for the day ahead
- Midday: Peace and guidance for current situations
- Evening: Gratitude and protection through the night

3. EMERGENCY PRAYER ORDER:

- "Jesus, I need You right now."
- Declare God's power over the situation.
- Pray specific Scripture promises
- Thank Him in advance for breakthrough

W - WORD-POWERED PRAYERS

Pray God's Promises Back to Him...

1. INSTEAD OF WORRIED PRAYERS, PRAY WORD-FILLED PRAYERS:

When You Feel...Pray This Scripture:

- *Anxious:* "God, Your peace guards my heart and mind" (Phil. 4:7)
- *Overwhelmed:* "I can do all things through Christ who strengthens me" (Phil. 4:13)
- *Lost:* "Your Word is a lamp to my feet and light to my path" (Psalm 119:105)
- *Afraid:* "You have not given me a spirit of fear, but of power, love, and a sound mind" (2 Tim. 1:7)
- *Discouraged:* "I will see Your goodness in the land of the living" (Psalm 27:13)

2. PERSONALIZE SCRIPTURE PRAYERS:

- *Insert names:* "Lord, help [child's name] trust You with all their heart"
- *Make it present:* "Right now, I declare that You are working all things together for my good."
- *Speak it with authority:* "In Jesus' name, I claim Your promise that..."

3. POWER VERSES:
- For Children: Proverbs 22:6, Psalm 127:3, 3 John 1:4
- For Marriage: Ecclesiastes 4:12, 1 Corinthians 13:4-7
- For Provision: Philippians 4:19, Matthew 6:26
- For Protection: Psalm 91, Psalm 23
- For Wisdom: James 1:5, Proverbs 3:5-6

E - EXPECT & ENGAGE

Pray with Faith and Take Action...

1. EXPECT GOD TO ANSWER:
- Pray with confidence, not desperation
- Look for answers in unexpected ways
- Document prayers and answers in a journal
- Thank God in advance for breakthrough

2. ENGAGE IN THE PROCESS:
- Listen for God's voice and direction
- Take practical steps alongside prayer
- Be patient with God's timing
- Stay persistent when answers seem delayed

3. FAITH-BUILDING PRACTICES:
- Pray and Act: Combine prayer with practical steps
- Pray and Wait: Trust God's timing for big decisions
- Pray and Watch: Look for God's hand in daily situations
- Pray and Worship: Celebrate answers when they come

4. SIGNS GOD IS ANSWERING:

- Unexplained peace in difficult situations
- Doors opening that were previously closed
- Wisdom and clarity in confusing circumstances
- Changed hearts (yours and others)
- Provision appears just when needed

R - REPEAT & RIPPLE

Build Consistency and Legacy...

1. REPEAT DAILY:
- Set consistent prayer times (even 5-10 minutes counts!)
- Use the same prayer spot to build a habit
- Pray through your household daily
- End each day with gratitude prayers

2. CREATE PRAYER RIPPLES:
- Teach others to pray (children, friends, family)
- Pray for people beyond your circle (community, nation, world)
- Document your prayer journey for future generations
- Share testimonies of answered prayers

3. WEEKLY PRAYER RHYTHMS:
- Monday: Pray for the week ahead
- Tuesday: Intercede for family and friends
- Wednesday: Pray for your community and nation
- Thursday: Spiritual warfare and breakthrough prayers
- Friday: Pray for your calling and future
- Saturday: Prayer for rest and restoration
- Sunday: Gratitude and worship prayers

4. LEGACY-BUILDING ACTIONS:
- Write prayers for your children's future
- Create family prayer traditions
- Pray for generational blessings
- Keep a prayer journal for posterity

CHAPTER 1

Why Most Prayers Feel Powerless (And How to Fix That)

The prayer of a righteous person is powerful and effective. —James 5:16 (NIV)

Last week, my friend Amara called me with her voice trembling.

"Marla, I've been praying for months about this situation. I've done everything I know to do. And still, nothing. I'm starting to wonder... is God even listening?"

I paused, letting her words settle. Because I've been there too. Maybe you have as well. You pour out your heart, but nothing seems to shift. You pray and pray, but doors stay closed. You whisper, "God, where are You?", and all you hear is silence. And in those moments, if you're not careful, doubt will creep in like a thief and convince you that your prayers are broken and ineffective.

But here's the truth I want to wrap around your heart today: it's not that God isn't listening; it's that many of us have been taught to pray like powerless people, not like the beloved, victorious daughters of the King that we are.

The Three Prayer Killers That Leave Us Spiritually Defeated

If you've ever felt like your prayers weren't working, it's not because God checked out. It may be time to check your approach. Let's talk about three common "prayer killers" that quietly sabotage *our faith*, and what to do instead.

Prayer Killer #1: The "Please, Pretty Please" Mentality

We tiptoe into prayer like we're interrupting God, apologizing as we

go:
- "God, if You're not too busy..."
- "I know I don't deserve this, but..."
- "If it's Your will..."

Of course we should honor God's sovereignty. But Scripture tells us to come boldly (Hebrews 4:16), not timidly. You wouldn't ask your earthly parent for food like a stranger hoping for scraps. You'd say, "Mama, I'm hungry." And guess what? Your Father in heaven welcomes that same boldness from you.

The Fix: Pray with the confidence of a child who knows she is deeply loved, and knows her Father will take care of her.

Prayer Killer #2: The "One and Done" Approach

We send up one prayer, and when nothing happens immediately, we assume the answer was no. But prayer isn't a microwave process; it's a slow crockpot, sometimes.

God honors persistence. Jesus Himself said to keep asking, keep seeking, and keep knocking (Matthew 7:7). He encouraged sincere, persistent prayer, not because God is ignoring you, but because faith grows in the waiting. When the answer to your prayer is revealed, you'll remember in your future how God showed up in the situation in the perfect way, at the perfect time.

The Fix: Keep praying until peace comes or the answer arrives. Persistence is not a lack of faith; it's a sign of it.

Prayer Killer #3: The "Hope So" Instead of "Know So" Faith

We say, "Lord, I hope You'll come through," while secretly bracing for disappointment. But faith is not a fragile wish; it's a firm belief. Powerful prayer doesn't beg; it believes. It doesn't waver in fear; it stands on what God already said.

The Fix: Anchor your prayers in the Word, not your feelings. God watches over His Word to perform it (Jeremiah 1:12), and that's not dependant on your emotions.

What Makes Prayer Powerful and Biblical

Real, biblical prayer isn't about checking a box. It's a spiritual transaction between heaven and earth. It's your access point to divine wisdom, supernatural breakthrough, and unshakable peace. Here's what sets powerful prayer apart:

1. Prayer Is Rooted in Relationship

God doesn't want polished speeches. He wants you. Prayer starts with presence. When you begin with worship and adoration, it realigns your heart to be aware of God's presence.

2. Prayer Is Anchored in the Word

When you pray Scripture, you're agreeing with what's already true in heaven, and calling it down to earth (Matthew 6:10). That kind of prayer gets results.

> *Your kingdom come, your will be done, on earth as it is in heaven.*
> — *Matthew 6:10, NIV*

3. Prayer Is Fueled by Gratitude

Gratitude isn't a bonus feature; it's a power source. Thanksgiving shifts your focus, returns you to an awareness of God's presence, builds your faith, and positions you to receive.

A Prayer That Changed Everything

Let me tell you about the prayer that changed the course of my life. One of my children was struggling. The kind of struggle that keeps a mother up at night. I prayed, oh, how I prayed. However, I finally realized that my prayers were full of fear and desperation, rather than faith.

So I opened my Bible to Isaiah 54:13: "All your children will be taught by the Lord, and great will be their peace." I stood on it. I spoke it aloud. I declared it like a warrior:

"Father, I thank You that [insert name] is taught by You. I bind anxiety, worry, and fear, and loose wisdom. I declare peace over [his/her] life, and I thank You that Your plans are still in place."

Two weeks later, that same child's whole demeanor and circumstances had changed, and their heart seemed lighter. That wasn't a coincidence. That was the power of praying God's Word. Sometimes, you may be the only one who truly sees how powerful God has moved in a situation because only you and God know just how bad it really was. When you see what you prayed about change, say "Thank You!", and move forward in joy, peace, and power.

The Blueprint: Jesus' Model Prayer

Jesus didn't say, "Here's a suggestion." He said, "This is how you should pray." (Matthew 6:9–13).

- *Our Father:* Identity and intimacy.
- *Hallowed be Your name:* Worship and reverence.
- *Your will be done:* Surrender and alignment.
- *Give us this day:* Provision and trust.
- *Forgive us:* Repentance and cleansing.
- *Deliver us:* Protection and authority.
- *For Yours is the kingdom:* Declaration and confidence

It's not a formula. It's a foundation. It provides the structure for you to build upon by specifically praying about what is on your heart, and what is occurring in your life, and the lives of your loved ones.

This Changes Everything

When you shift your prayers from panic to purpose, from begging to believing, from passive to powerful, you're no longer a bystander in your own life. You're a co-laborer with God. And the enemy? He knows it.

Your words carry weight. Your prayers carry authority. You don't have to wonder if you're being heard, you are. You don't have to hope things will change; you can pray knowing they already are.

A Declaration to Pray Right Now

"Father, I thank You that You have given me authority through Jesus Christ. I refuse to pray small, powerless prayers. I choose to pray boldly, anchored in Your Word. I believe You hear me. I expect You to move. My prayers are powerful and effective, because I am Your daughter, and You delight in answering me. In Jesus' Name, Amen."

Prayer Assessment Quiz: "Where Am I in My Prayer Life?"

This quick self-check is designed to help you reflect on how you currently approach prayer. There are no right or wrong answers, just an honest space to locate yourself before God and get excited about how far He's going to take you!

For each statement, choose the answer that feels most true for you:

1. I feel confident that God hears me when I pray.
A) Always
B) Sometimes
C) Rarely

2. I pray consistently throughout my week.
A) Daily
B) A few times a week
C) Only when things get really hard

3. I include worship, thanksgiving, and Scripture in my prayers.
A) Often
B) Occasionally
C) Not really

4. I pray expecting God to move.
A) Yes, every time
B) I try to
C) Honestly, I hope, but I'm not sure

5. I've seen answers to my prayers.
A) Many
B) A few
C) I'm still waiting

How to Reflect on Your Score:

- Mostly A's: You're building a strong prayer life! Keep going; you're growing in faith and power.
- Mostly B's: You're in the middle of a breakthrough season. God is drawing you closer. Stay engaged.
- Mostly C's: This is your turning point. Don't be discouraged; this book will help you shift from confusion to confidence.

Reflection Questions

Take time to journal or simply talk with the Lord about your answers:

1. What has shaped your current view of prayer: past experiences, church traditions, personal struggles?
2. When was the last time you felt truly heard by God? What made that moment different?
3. What would your ideal prayer life look like if you removed guilt, fear, and doubt?
4. Which "Prayer Killer" spoke the loudest to you, and how can you begin shifting it today?
5. What is one Scripture you can begin praying daily this week to renew your faith?

Tip: Use your *Enhancing Your Journey: 90-Day Prayer Journal* to record your reflections and begin building a deeper, more consistent rhythm.

Closing Prayer for You

Father,

I thank You for the woman holding this book in her hands right now. You know her heart. You know her fears, her frustrations, and her deepest hopes. I speak life over her prayer life today. Let every feeling of inadequacy, silence, or uncertainty be replaced with boldness, clarity, and peace.

Lord, teach her to pray not from a place of begging but from her position as Your beloved daughter. Open her ears to hear Your whispers. Open her eyes to see Your hand moving. Let her confidence rise, not because of her perfection, but because of Your promises.

I declare that she will pray with fire, with faith, and with full expectation. Her prayers will shift atmospheres, strengthen her household, and leave a legacy of faith for generations. I thank You, Lord, that this is her moment, her season to go deeper, to rise up, and to step fully into the authority You've given her.

In the mighty Name of Jesus, Amen.

CHAPTER 2

The Life-Changing Power of Prayer (And Why the World Needs You to Use It)

What is Prayer?

At its core, prayer is simply communication with God. It's a conversation; not a formal presentation, not a wish list, but an open, honest dialogue between you and your Creator. God is always with us, and prayer simply allows us to talk to Him along our life journey. Prayer is a sacred exchange where we talk to God, listen for His voice, and align our hearts with His will. It's the privilege of every believer, a direct line to the King of Kings, no appointment necessary.

As a mother, I often think about how my children come to me. Sometimes they need advice, sometimes they just want to be near me, and other times they have come running full-speed because something went wrong. That's how our relationship with God should be: unfiltered, unpolished, and full of trust and confidence that He is always there desiring to love, comfort, guide, and help us.

Why is Prayer Essential in a Believer's Life?

Prayer isn't just a spiritual discipline; it's the foundation of our faith. The Bible tells us to "pray without ceasing" (1 Thessalonians 5:17, NKJV), meaning that prayer should be woven into every part of our lives, no matter how we feel or what circumstances we are facing. Why? Because prayer:

- **Strengthens our relationship with God:** "Draw near to God, and He will draw near to you." — James 4:8, NKJV

- **Brings peace in the midst of chaos:** "Be anxious for nothing, but in everything by prayer and supplication, with thanksgiving, let your requests be made known to God; and the peace of God, which surpasses all understanding, will guard your hearts and minds through Christ Jesus." — Philippians 4:6-7, NKJV

- **Gives us wisdom and direction:** "Trust in the Lord with all your heart and lean not on your own understanding; in all your ways submit to Him, and He will make your paths straight." — Proverbs 3:5-6 NIV.

  "The wise will hear and increase their learning, And the person of understanding will acquire wise counsel and the skill [to steer his course wisely and lead others to the truth]," — Proverbs 1:5, AMP

- **Empowers us to overcome obstacles:** "Truly I tell you, if anyone says to this mountain, 'Go, throw yourself into the sea,' and does not doubt in their heart but believes that what they say will happen, it will be done for them." — Mark 11:23 NIV.

For these reasons, our lives should be filled with frequent, spontaneous prayer. Praying without ceasing helps us to remember to depend on God and to do God's will, gives us a new perspective concerning challenges, and helps us to remain more joyful and thankful in our everyday lives.

The prayer of a righteous person is powerful and effective. —*James 5:16 (NIV)*

When one of my sons was around four years old, he looked up at me and asked the most unexpected question: "Mommy, why do you always talk to someone I can't see?"

I stopped mid-stir at the stove, spoon in hand, and smiled. In that moment, I realized something profound: my son had been watching me pray during everyday moments, while cooking dinner, folding laundry, buckling seatbelts, and navigating the beautiful chaos of family life. To him, I wasn't practicing religion. I was demonstrating relationship.

Prayer wasn't something I taught him with words; it was something he witnessed with his eyes. And that's when it hit me: Prayer isn't just about what happens when we pray; it's about who we become because we pray.

More Than a Conversation

Prayer is more than a conversation with God; it's a lifeline. It's the invisible cord that connects our everyday to eternity, our problems to God's power, our limitations to His limitless grace.

When you pray, you're not releasing words into thin air; you're releasing power into your atmosphere. You're activating angelic reinforcements, opening the gates of wisdom, and inviting the supernatural into your natural circumstances.

Let me say it plainly: Prayer is your divine advantage. It's how you access:

- Spiritual breath: Prayer keeps your spirit alive and alert.
- Divine downloads: Guidance that goes beyond human logic.
- Heaven's authority: Power to bind, loose, declare, and cover.
- Peace that transcends: No matter what's happening externally.
- Miraculous intervention: God's response to your real-time need.

Why Prayer Is Not Optional for Every Believer

1. Prayer Connects You to the Source: Just like a phone without a charger eventually dies, a life without prayer slowly runs out of power. Prayer keeps you aligned with the One who holds it all.

2. Prayer Activates Heaven on Earth: Your prayers are not just heard; they're answered. You're not begging; you're partnering. When you pray according to God's will, things begin to shift. (1 John 5:14-15)

3. Prayer Protects What Matters Most: Your prayers cover your children, strengthen your marriage, bless your home, and put a shield of favor over your life. You may not see it in the moment, but heaven records every word.

Biblical Examples When Prayer Caused God to Respond, and Proved That Prayer Changes Everything:

Let's revisit just a few moments in Scripture where ordinary people dared to pray and heaven responded.

1. Hannah's Prayer for a Child: 1 Samuel 1:10–20

In deep anguish, Hannah wept and prayed fervently for a child. God heard her prayer and gave her Samuel, who became one of Israel's greatest prophets. Hannah didn't settle for heartbreak. She poured out her soul, and God gave her Samuel, a prophet whose voice helped shape a nation.

Key theme: Prayer through grief and longing brings life-changing breakthrough.

2. Elijah's Prayer for Rain: 1 Kings 18:41-45

After a long drought, Elijah continued to pray persistently for rain. His faith-filled prayers brought clouds and a mighty downpour. Elijah didn't stop at one prayer. He kept praying until he saw a cloud the size of a man's hand, and God sent rain that ended a years-long drought.

Key theme: Persistent prayer shifts atmospheres and ends dry seasons. Continue praying until you see what God says.

3. The Prayer of Jabez: 1 Chronicles 4:10

Jabez boldly asked God to enlarge his territory and keep him from harm, and "God granted his request."

Key theme: Bold prayers aligned with purpose receive God's favor.

4. Hezekiah's Prayer for Healing: 2 Kings 20:1–6

When the prophet Isaiah told Hezekiah he would die, the king turned his face to the wall and prayed. God added 15 years to his life.

Key theme: Honest, urgent prayer can rewrite what appears to be the final outcome.

5. Jehoshaphat's Prayer in Crisis: 2 Chronicles 20:1-30

Facing overwhelming enemies, Jehoshaphat prayed and declared, "We do not know what to do, but our eyes are on You." God responded with miraculous victory through worship.

Key theme: Humble prayer in crisis invites divine strategy and supernatural rescue.

6. Daniel's Prayer for Revelation: Daniel 9:1-23

Daniel fasted and prayed for understanding. While he was still praying, the angel Gabriel arrived with divine insight.

Key theme: Prayer opens the heavens and releases answers from God's throne.

7. The Early Church's Prayer for Boldness: Acts 4:23-31

After being threatened, the early believers prayed for courage to speak God's Word. The place shook, and they were filled with the Holy Spirit.

Key theme: Unified prayer empowers boldness and divine confirmation.

8. Peter's Miraculous Escape from Prison: Acts 12:5-17

While Peter was imprisoned, the church prayed earnestly for him. An angel appeared, broke his chains, and led him to freedom. When Peter was imprisoned, the church didn't panic; they prayed. And God sent an angel who walked Peter right out of that prison. Chains broke. Doors opened. Miracles happened.

Key theme: Intercessory prayer releases the miraculous and defies impossibility.

9. Jesus' Prayer in Gethsemane: Luke 22:39-46

Jesus prayed fervently before His arrest, surrendering His will to the Father. Strength was given to fulfill His mission.

Key theme: Prayer in pain produces power for purpose. Nothing truly great has ever been done without some form of pain or sacrifice.

10. Cornelius' Prayer Opens the Door to the Gentiles: Acts 10:1–4

Cornelius' consistent prayer and giving moved heaven. God sent Peter with the message of salvation, opening the door to Gentile believers.

Key theme: Persistent prayer prepares hearts and shifts spiritual history.

A Modern-Day Miracle in My Own Home

Not long ago, my husband experienced multiple strokes which resulted in multiple hospital stays. As a wife and mother, it crushed me. I couldn't fix it. But I could pray. And that's precisely what I, and many others who know our family, did.

For weeks, we declared Scripture. We spoke life. We refused to accept the enemy's report. And when the final test results came in, within weeks, my husband was released from the hospital and physical and occupational therapy as well. He was up walking, talking, and living again. While we still have some challenges to overcome, the doctors and nurses even called him a miracle. We called it all God.

The Authority You Carry in Prayer

If you only knew what happens when you pray, you'd never stop. Jesus didn't just invite you to pray; He authorized you to pray. You carry heaven's authority.

1. **You have power over fear:** "For God has not given us a spirit of fear, but of power and of love and of a sound mind." — 2 Timothy 1:7, NKJV.
2. **You have the ability to bind and loose:** "Assuredly, I say to you, whatever you bind on earth will be bound in heaven, and whatever you loose on earth will be loosed in heaven." — Matthew 18:18, NKJV.
3. **You are more than a conqueror:** "Yet in all these things we are more than conquerors through Him who loved us." — Romans 8:37, NKJV

Prayer: Your Secret Weapon for Everyday Life
- Prayer isn't reserved for crises. It's your moment-by-moment

power source.

- Praying over your children is not routine; it's legacy-building.
- Praying in the kitchen isn't multitasking; it's hosting heaven in your home.
- Praying in tension isn't stalling; it's silencing the enemy with wisdom and peace.

Every time you pray, you shift the atmosphere. And when a woman shifts the atmosphere in her home, she changes the trajectory of her family.

The Ripple Effect of a Praying Life

When you commit to a life of prayer:

- Peace replaces panic
- Wisdom replaces confusion
- Power replaces passivity
- Miracles replace despair

Your life becomes a beacon, inviting others to seek the God you talk to daily.

Your Assignment

God placed you in your family, workplace, and community on purpose. You are His ambassador. His intercessor. His change agent. Don't underestimate what happens when you pray. Because the world doesn't need more people speaking and making noise, it needs more people who pray.

Reflection Questions

1. When have you seen God answer your prayers in unexpected ways?
2. What does it mean to you that prayer is not just communication, but activation?
3. How can you begin to see your daily prayers as spiritually strategic?
4. What's one area in your life where you need to take back your authority in prayer?

5. Who in your life needs covering, and how can you begin interceding for them today?

Prayer to Declare

Father,

Thank You for the life-changing power of prayer. Thank You that I have direct access to You, not because of what I've done, but because of who You are. Today, I choose to step into my authority as Your daughter. I refuse to pray weak prayers. I declare Your Word over my life and my home. Let Your power be activated through me. Use my prayers to shift atmospheres, break chains, bring healing, and release hope. I commit to partnering with You, not just to survive, but to bring heaven to earth through bold, believing, Spirit-filled prayer.

In Jesus' Name, Amen.

CHAPTER 3

How to Pray, Lessons from the Lord's Prayer

This, then, is how you should pray... – Matthew 6:9 (NIV)

When Prayer Feels Like a Foreign Language

It was 2 a.m. I was pacing the kitchen in my pajamas. My husband was out of town, and the relationship between us wasn't feeling too great. I felt disconnected from him and overwhelmed with the task of caring for my family. After a day of errands, extra curricular events and activities of our children, and making sure the family was fed, the dishes were piled high. And I honestly couldn't remember the last time I'd taken time to care for my mind, my body, or my spirit.

Right there, in the middle of the exhaustion and emptiness, I whispered: "God, I need help. But I don't even know how to ask anymore."

Maybe you've been there too: so stretched, so tired, so overwhelmed that even your prayers feel like one more thing you can't get right. That's exactly why Jesus gave us a prayer model, not a script to recite mindlessly, but a powerful blueprint for real-life, real-time conversations with God.

The Lord's Prayer in Matthew 6:9–13 is more than tradition. It's a timeless structure for prayer.

It's for the mom doing school drop-offs.

It's for the woman holding it all together.

It's for you.

Let's walk through it together, one verse at a time, and see how this divine framework can strengthen your prayer life, reset your heart, and re-mind you that God is closer than you think.

After this manner therefore pray ye:

Our Father which art in heaven,
Hallowed be thy name.
Thy kingdom come, Thy will be done in earth, as it is in heaven.
Give us this day our daily bread.
And forgive us our debts, as we forgive our debtors.
And lead us not into temptation, but deliver us from evil:
For thine is the kingdom, and the power, and the glory, for ever.
Amen.
— Matthew 6:9-13, KJV

"Our Father in Heaven": Approaching God as a Loving Father

When my kids come to me, they don't schedule an appointment or come with perfect words. They just come with all their needs, stories, and messes.

That's what Jesus was teaching us when He opened the prayer with "Our Father." This is intimate language: personal, safe, and welcoming. He's not just God of the universe, He's your Father. You don't have to impress Him. You just have to show up.

Try This: Begin your next prayer with "Daddy" or "Papa" instead of "Lord" and notice how your heart softens.

"Hallowed Be Your Name": The Power of Praise, Reverence, and Worship in Prayer

Worship isn't about ignoring your problems but about remembering your God. It's about acknowledging and returning to an awareness of His presence with you right now.

One morning, everything was going wrong: the washing machine broke, the car wouldn't start, and one of my kids had a meltdown over cereal. I wanted to cry, but I chose to praise. I said, "God, You're still good. You're still in control." And peace settled over my soul like a warm blanket.

When you start with worship, you stop being consumed by what's wrong and start being reminded of who God is: Provider, Healer, Defender, Friend. Whatever is happening, return your focus to God. Doing so restores peace and order to the situation, providing you with the strength to get through it.

Praise changes our perspective. I've learned that no matter how chaotic my day is, taking a moment to praise God shifts everything. Worshipping always reminds me that He has never left or forsaken me (Hebrews 13:5). It reminds me that it is my responsibility to return to an awareness of His amazing, loving presence. When I worship, God inhabits my praise (Psalm 22:3).

Along with experiencing blessings to praise God for, I've had many reasons to cry throughout my life: the deaths of loved ones, the death of my mother at an early age, loss, betrayal by friends and loved ones, my loved ones facing illnesses, facing sickness myself, failure to accomplish goals and dreams in the timing I desired, my children experiencing hurt or loss, and feeling like I have lost hope for various other reasons.

However, throughout my life, as I have cried out to God for help, He has always provided help in His perfect way and at the perfect time. I am a witness that worship reminds us that God is with us. It reminds us about who God is: our Provider, our Healer, our Refuge (Psalm 100:4). When we start prayer with reverence and acknowledge all that God has done and all He has seen us through, it transforms our worries into worship and strengthens our faith for what is to come.

Try This: Turn on one worship song each morning before you check your phone or email. Let that be your reset.

"Your Kingdom Come, Your Will Be Done": Seeking God's Will Above Our Own

As a mom, wife, coach, and multitasker, I love having a plan. But I've learned that holding tight to my own agenda only leads to frustration. Having a household of nine people, nine personalities and nine separate schedules for over 25 years makes it very challenging to have a regular schedule to accomplish any plan. Praying for God's will, and really meaning it, has brought more peace than any to-do list ever could.

Praying for God's will to be done requires trusting that He sees me, and sees what I can't. That His way is better. That surrender is not weakness; it's wisdom.

Let's be real, surrender isn't easy, especially when you're juggling schedules, finances, personalities, and the needs of a family. However, trusting God's plan and leaning on Him with our full weight always leads to greater peace (Proverbs 3:5-6).

As we live with dependence on God, He will keep us on course to achieve our purpose and destiny. When we pray for His Kingdom to come and bring our decision-making process to Him, we align ourselves with His purpose and ask for His rule and reign to be evident in our lives, our communities, and our world.

God's design, plan, and purpose for our life will always be better and bigger than our own (Ephesians 3:20). Turn every area of your life over to God, surrender to His plan, and trust Him to guide and protect you on your journey.

Prayer Framework for Surrender:
- "God, here's what I want..."
- "But I trust You know what I need..."
- "Help me release this into Your hands."
- I've made my request, completely believing what You have promised and can fulfill, and I'm leaving it at Your altar.
- Thank You for Your Kingdom coming and your perfect will being done, in Jesus' name, Amen.

"Give Us This Day Our Daily Bread": Trusting God to Provide

I've had to lean on God's provision more times than I can count. I've stood in front of an empty pantry and a jam-packed calendar, wondering how everything would come together, and somehow, He always made a way. Whether it was unexpected groceries on the doorstep, a surprise gift card in the mail, a timely word of encouragement, or inner strength I didn't know I had, God showed up. Again and again, He reminded me that He cares about every part of our daily needs: emotional, physical, financial, and spiritual.

He wants us to ask. He wants us to trust. And it's often in the pressures and unpredictability of life that we learn just how faithful He truly is. Those moments of depending on Him for our "daily bread" don't just sustain us, they teach us who He is. They reveal His heart, His reliability, and the depth of His care. And as we experience His provision firsthand, we begin to know, not just believe, that we can trust Him completely.

Provision looks different for everyone. Sometimes, it's about food on the table; other times, it's about emotional strength to get through a tough day. God is our sustainer and provider (Philippians 4:19), and when we bring our needs before Him, He meets them in ways beyond what we could imagine.

I implore you to pray about everything, from the smallest to the most significant matters. I've faced numerous challenges in life that God has brought me through, and I know that I know God has got me. And as you trust Him, He's got you too.

Whether our needs are physical, mental, emotional, or spiritual, we are to trust God for our daily nourishment. And trust that He knows what is best and that He will provide exactly what He knows we need, exactly when we need it. He's truly intentional and never fails. Ask, and trust Him to provide.

For this reason I am telling you, whatever things you ask for in prayer {in accordance with God's will}, believe {with confident trust} that you have received them, and they will be given to you. —Mark 11:24, AMP

Try This: Each morning, write down one thing you need today, and give it to God before you try to fix it yourself.

"Forgive Us Our Debts", Living Free Through Grace and Forgiveness

Forgiveness isn't easy, but it's essential. It stretches the heart, confronts our pride, and invites God to heal the places we'd rather forget. It's not a one-time lesson; it's a daily, deliberate choice to live free.

I'll never forget the time I completely lost my patience with one of my teenage sons. It had been a long, exhausting day, and he made a small mistake that, in the moment, felt enormous. I snapped: harsh words, sharp tone, more frustration than the situation deserved. And while I felt justified at first, conviction came fast. That still, small voice whispered, "Go make it right."

So I did. I walked into his room, sat on the edge of his bed, and with tears in my eyes said, "I was wrong. I'm sorry. Will you forgive me?" And he did.

In that moment, healing entered the room, not just for him, but for me too. We both grew. We both softened. That's the power of grace.

Forgiveness isn't about pretending the hurt didn't happen. It's about releasing it to the One who can carry it. It's about choosing freedom over bitterness, peace over pride, and love over offense.

Coming from a big family, navigating marriage, and raising a house full of kids, I've learned something firsthand: unforgiveness poisons the atmosphere. Grudges create distance. Silent tension erodes connection. But forgiveness? Forgiveness heals. It humbles. It restores.

God calls us to a lifestyle of grace because we've been lavished with grace ourselves. "Forgive, just as the Lord forgave you" (Colossians 3:13). When we forgive, we reflect His heart. We model compassion, humility, patience, and quiet strength, the kind of qualities that not only change us but can change the culture of our homes, workplaces, and communities.

But here's the truth: forgiveness starts with the inside work. It begins with letting God deal with our hearts: our hurt, our pride, our need for control. Holding onto resentment has never helped anyone. Bitterness only builds walls where God wants to restore bridges.

I often encourage what I call "rapid forgiveness", a practice of choosing to release offense as quickly as it comes. That doesn't mean staying in toxic or abusive situations. Wisdom and boundaries matter. But it does mean refusing to nurse anger, replay the offense, or allow negativity to take root.

We forgive because we remember how deeply we've been forgiven. We let go because we trust God to lift us forward. And we lead with love, even when it's hard, especially when it's hard.

Forgiveness is not a favor you give the other person. It's freedom you give yourself. And that freedom makes room for God to move in ways you never imagined.

Try This: Ask yourself: "Is there someone I need to forgive, or someone I need to ask forgiveness from today?"

Don't wait. Whether it's a whisper between you and God or a conversation with someone else, take the first step. Let it go. Then let God and His grace do the work.

For as the heavens are higher than the earth, so are My ways higher than your ways, and My thoughts than your thoughts. — Isaiah 55:9, NKJV

"Lead Us Not Into Temptation", Asking for Strength in the Struggle

Temptation doesn't always come in dramatic moments or obvious sins. For women, and for those who are mothers, it often shows up in subtler forms:

- The urge to snap when we're exhausted.
- The pull to compare when we're insecure.
- The instinct to control when we feel out of control.

- The drift toward fear when trust feels hard.

These temptations are real. They sneak into everyday life between laundry piles, behind deadlines, through hurtful words, or in quiet disappointments. And if we're not spiritually anchored, they can wear us down before we even realize what's happening.

But here's the hope: prayer is your resistance plan. It's where we gather strength to rise above emotional reactions and spiritual fatigue. It's where we ask God to guard our minds, steady our hearts, and help us walk in victory, one moment at a time.

Over the years, I've learned to lean on what I call "breath prayers": short, honest whispers that invite God into the middle of the moment:

- "Lord, help me speak gently."
- "Jesus, be my peace right now."
- "Holy Spirit, take over."

These quick prayers are like spiritual oxygen in the chaos. They're small, but mighty. And sometimes, they're the only thing keeping me grounded when everything feels like it's spinning.

Why We Must Pray for Strength Daily

Temptation shows up in many forms:

- The temptation to worry instead of trust
- To give up when things feel too heavy
- To lash out when we feel misunderstood
- To lean into distraction instead of devotion

That's why Jesus included this line in His model prayer, because He knew we'd need it. "Lead us not into temptation..." is both a plea for guidance and a request for supernatural strength.

Scripture says, "Put on the full armor of God, so that you can take your stand against the devil's schemes" (Ephesians 6:11, NIV). God never intended for us to fight battles unarmed. He's given us truth, righteousness, peace, faith, salvation, and His Word; not as nice ideas, but as daily protection against very real spiritual warfare (Ephesians 6:10–18 AMP).

But armor isn't useful unless you put it on. And for me? That happens in prayer.

Prayer as a Lifeline, Not a Last Resort

As a woman who wears many hats, mother, wife, daughter, sister, leader, and coach. I've had to make prayer my habit, not my afterthought. It's not just something I do when life falls apart. It's the rhythm that holds me together.

I've prayed through tears while wiping little faces. I've whispered prayers while driving to meetings and folding laundry. Some days my prayers are long and deep. Other days, they're short and desperate. Either way, they are real.

Each day brings its own battles, some loud and obvious, others subtle and heavy. But I've discovered that when I stay connected to God, I stay standing. And not just standing, I'm strengthened. "Pray without ceasing" (1 Thessalonians 5:17) has become more than a Bible verse. It has become a lifeline.

Let Prayer Be Your Reset and Your Strength

You don't need perfect words. You don't need eloquence. What you need is consistency, small, honest conversations with the One who already knows and understands.

Let prayer become the sacred thread woven through your day:

- A whisper in the grocery aisle
- A pause in the car line
- A sigh at the kitchen sink
- A deep breath before you respond

These moments matter. They keep your spirit grounded, your heart open, and your mind steady. They equip you, not just to endure, but to overcome.

Try This: Create your own "go-to prayer" for difficult moments: something short, powerful, and personal.

Write it on a sticky note and place it on your mirror, dashboard, or phone screen. Speak it aloud when frustration rises, when fear creeps in, or when you're simply feeling overwhelmed.

Examples:

- "God, I choose peace over panic."
- "Lord, steady my thoughts and soften my words."
- "Jesus, remind me that You are near."

"Deliver Us from Evil", Protection in the Middle of the Battle

"Deliver us from evil…"

Those four words aren't just a line in a prayer. They are a cry of the heart from every woman who has ever faced hardship, heartache, or spiritual attack and still chose to stand in faith.

- If you've ever felt like darkness was closing in…
- If you've ever sat in a car crying, wondering how you're going to make it through the next hour…
- If you've ever been surrounded by people but felt completely unseen or misunderstood…
- If you've battled fear, anxiety, betrayal, or loss, and still tried to keep your family, your faith, and your mind intact…

Then you know what it means to need deliverance. Because evil isn't always a shadowy figure. It often looks like:

- The lingering effects of childhood trauma
- The constant barrage of negative thoughts
- Generational cycles of poverty, addiction, or dysfunction
- The aftermath of infidelity
- The manipulation of a toxic relationship
- A spirit of fear that tries to paralyze you at every step

But here's the truth I want to remind you of: God sees it. God knows. God delivers. And God restores.

The Battle Is Real, But So Is Your Defender

We are not wrestling against flesh and blood, but against spiritual forces of darkness (Ephesians 6:12). That means the battle you're facing isn't just physical, it's spiritual. And while you may feel weak or weary, you are not fighting alone.

God doesn't expect you to be your own protector. He wants to be your refuge, your shield, your strong tower. When you pray "deliver me from evil," you're not just asking for escape, you're inviting God to step in with divine power and push back everything that's been pushing against you.

He is your:

- Defender when your name is being slandered
- Protector when your children are under spiritual attack
- Restorer when your marriage is broken
- Peace when your mind feels like a war zone
- Healer when your body or heart is worn down

When the Fight Is Too Much, God Fights For You

There have been seasons where I felt like I had no strength left to fight, times when the enemy was whispering lies, my emotions were frayed, and my prayers felt weak. But I've learned that even when I'm too tired to stand, God never stops fighting for me.

You may be going through a spiritual battle right now. It may be one no one else sees, one you've had to cry through in silence. But hear me clearly, sis: You are not powerless. And you are not alone.

God is your deliverer. He breaks chains. He silences storms. He restores what was stolen. He lifts you from the pit and places you back on solid ground. He will never leave you defenseless.

Try This: A Prayer for Protection and Deliverance

"Father, You are my defender and my shield. I ask You today to deliver me from everything that threatens my peace, seen and unseen. Break every chain, silence every lie, and destroy every assignment of the enemy over my life, my family, my finances, my mind, and my future. I refuse to walk in fear, because You are with me. Surround me with Your angels, fill my heart with Your truth, and lead me forward in freedom. I declare that I am protected, covered, and delivered by the power of Your name.

In Jesus' name, Amen."

Reflect and Respond

- Where do you feel like the enemy is attacking you the most right now, your peace, your relationships, your confidence?
- Have you been trying to fight in your own strength?
- What would it look like to hand that battle back to God today?

Write down one scripture about God's protection and keep it in a visible place this week. Here are a few to choose from.

Scriptures on God's Protection

Protection from Fear & Danger:
- Psalm 91:1-2 (NIV): "Whoever dwells in the shelter of the Most High will rest in the shadow of the Almighty. I will say of the Lord, 'He is my refuge and my fortress, my God, in whom I trust.'"
- Isaiah 41:10 (NIV): "So do not fear, for I am with you; do not be dismayed, for I am your God. I will strengthen you and help you; I will uphold you with my righteous right hand."
- Proverbs 18:10 (NIV): "The name of the Lord is a fortified tower; the righteous run to it and are safe."

Divine Protection in Battle:
- Ephesians 6:11 (AMP): "Put on the full armor of God [for His precepts are like the splendid armor of a heavily-armed soldier], so that you may be able to successfully stand up against all the schemes and the strategies and the deceits of the devil."
- 2 Thessalonians 3:3 (NIV): "But the Lord is faithful, and he will strengthen you and protect you from the evil one."
- Psalm 34:7 (NIV): "The angel of the Lord encamps around those who fear him, and he delivers them."

Protection Over Family & Children:
- Isaiah 54:13 (NIV): "All your children will be taught by the Lord, and great will be their peace."

- Psalm 121:7-8 (NIV): "The Lord will keep you from all harm—he will watch over your life; the Lord will watch over your coming and going both now and forevermore."
- Psalm 91:11 (NIV): "For he will command his angels concerning you to guard you in all your ways."

Protection in the Unknown:
- Deuteronomy 31:6 (NIV): "Be strong and courageous. Do not be afraid or terrified because of them, for the Lord your God goes with you; he will never leave you nor forsake you."
- Exodus 14:14 (NIV): "The Lord will fight for you; you need only to be still."
- Isaiah 43:2 (NIV): "When you pass through the waters, I will be with you; and when you pass through the rivers, they will not sweep over you. When you walk through the fire, you will not be burned; the flames will not set you ablaze."

"Yours Is the Kingdom, Power, and Glory", Ending in Confidence and Praise

There's something sacred about how we end a prayer. Not with a sigh of defeat, but with a shout of confidence. When we declare, "Yours is the kingdom, the power, and the glory, forever," we are doing more than closing a conversation. We're lifting our eyes from the chaos of earth to the certainty of heaven.

We're choosing praise over panic.
We're declaring truth in the middle of uncertainty.
We're reminding our hearts who's really in control.

Prayer doesn't always change our circumstances instantly, but it always changes us. And when we end our prayers in worship, we anchor ourselves in the unshakable character of God. He is still reigning, still ruling, and still redeeming, even when we can't see how just yet.

I've made it a habit to close my prayers with this simple but bold declaration: "God, I fully believe and trust You to do what only You can do."

And friend, I can tell you from experience that trust, even when whispered through tears, is enough. That faith, even when fragile, moves the heart of God. And that surrender, even when trembling, is worship at its purest.

Why Praise Matters at the End

Ending your prayers in praise isn't about pretending everything is perfect. It's about proclaiming that God is. It's about resting in the truth that, no matter what you face today, God's kingdom still stands, His power is still active, and His glory will still shine.

When you say "Yours is the kingdom," you're releasing control and acknowledging that His ways are higher. When you say "Yours is the power," you're admitting that your strength has limits, but His does not. When you say "Yours is the glory," you're surrendering the outcome and trusting Him to work all things together for your good, even the things that broke your heart.

As Revelation 5:13 reminds us, "To Him who sits on the throne and to the Lamb be praise and honor and glory and power, for ever and ever!" That truth doesn't expire when life gets hard. If anything, it becomes more vital.

We Win Because He Reigns

The story of your life is still being written, but here's what you can know for sure: God reigns. His kingdom is unshakable. His plans are unstoppable. And His love for you is unchanging.

He's not pacing the floors of heaven wondering what to do next. He's working, healing, guiding, and delivering behind the scenes. Every time you choose to close your prayer in faith, you're building spiritual muscle. You're growing in maturity. And you're saying, "I trust You, Lord, more than I trust what I see."

So worship Him at the end. Praise Him before the answer arrives. And trust that because of His great love, you can walk forward with confidence.

Chapter Recap: Key Takeaways

The Lord's Prayer isn't just words to repeat. It's a divine invitation into honest, powerful communication with God. Every line invites you into deeper connection: to worship, surrender, receive, forgive, stand firm, and ultimately rest in God's authority.

You don't need perfect phrasing, just a heart that's willing. Prayer is your lifeline, your secret weapon, and your daily reset. Start with reverence.

End with confidence. Let the middle be honest and raw. This is where transformation happens.

Reflection Questions

1. Which part of the Lord's Prayer speaks most directly to your heart right now?
2. Are there areas of your life where you've struggled to let go and fully trust God?
3. How does acknowledging God's power and kingdom change the way you see your current struggle?
4. What's one way you can begin ending your prayers with greater faith and boldness?

Prayer to Declare

Heavenly Father,

Thank You for inviting me into conversation with You, not because I have it all together, but because You do. Help me to pray with boldness, to trust when it's hard, and to praise even when it's painful. I want to walk in full surrender, resting in Your wisdom and love. I declare that Yours is the kingdom, Yours is the power, and Yours is the glory over my life, my family, my future, and my every day. I trust You to move in ways only You can.

In Jesus' powerful Name, Amen.

CHAPTER 4

The Different Types of Prayer

Prayer is not a one-size-fits-all conversation with God. Just as my children come to me for different reasons, sometimes for comfort, sometimes for advice, and sometimes just to be close. Our prayers can take on different forms depending on our needs. The Bible shows us many ways to pray. Each serving a unique purpose in drawing us closer to God and strengthening our faith. Let's explore these different types of prayer and how we can apply them powerfully in our lives.

1. A Prayer of Worship: Simply Loving on God

Come, let us bow down in worship, let us kneel before the Lord our Maker, for he is our God and we are the people of His pasture, the flock under His care.
— Psalm 95:6–7, NIV

Sweet friend, worship isn't just something we do on Sunday morning or during our favorite song. Worship is a posture of the heart. It's not about asking for anything; it's about pouring love back onto the God who so freely gives it.

Think about how your child gazes at you with those wide, trusting eyes when they're filled with love and wonder. That's the kind of heart posture God longs for from us in worship; pure, surrendered, and in awe of who He is. Not for what He can do but simply because of who He has always been.

Worship re-centers your soul. It's the moment when the noise of your busy day fades away and your spirit whispers, "God, You are good." It's in that sacred space, whether you're folding laundry, running errands, driving from work or to school pickup, or kneeling quietly before Him, that your heart begins to shift from chaos to calm, from fear to faith.

Worship doesn't require perfection. You don't need the right words, the right setting, or the perfect voice. You just need a heart that chooses to honor God, even in the mess. When you choose to worship, when you lift your hands, whisper a "thank You," or simply sit in silence with Him, you create space for Him to move in your life. And He will move, sis.

When you worship, you're saying, "Lord, I trust You more than my fear. I surrender my timeline, my desires, and my questions. I believe You're in control, and I give You the highest place in my heart." It realigns your perspective. It reminds you that He is God, and you are not required to carry everything alone. It softens the hard places, ignites your faith, and awakens your spirit to the truth that He is working even when you don't see it yet.

Worship isn't just a spiritual discipline; it's your lifeline. It opens the door for God's peace to enter your chaos and for His wisdom to replace your worry. And when you make space to simply love on God for who He is, not just what He can do, your faith grows deeper, richer, and stronger.

So as you go about your day, loving your family, running your home, and pursuing your purpose. Pause often and lift your heart in worship. Even in whispered moments, He hears you. Let your life be a love letter to the Father. Let your worship remind you that you are seen, loved, and held by the One who never lets go.

2. Confession Prayer, When You Need to Own It and Let Grace In

If we confess our sins, He is faithful and just and will forgive us our sins and purify us from all unrighteousness. — *1 John 1:9, NIV*

Confession is not about guilt trips or shame spirals; it's about freedom. It's the moment you stop hiding and pretending, and start healing. It's the honest breath that says, "God, I missed it. And I need You."

Confession isn't weakness; it's strength. It builds connection. It opens the door to healing. And it models the very grace we all so desperately need.

Sin isn't just about rules broken; it's about a relationship broken. It creates distance. It clogs the pipeline between us and God, making everything feel a little heavier, a little colder. And it can do the same thing in our relationships with others we care about. But confession? It clears the debris. It says, "God, I want to be close again."

God already knows where we've fallen short. What He desires is our honesty, our humility, and our willingness to let Him in. And just like we would welcome our children back into our arms with open hearts and no hesitation, He receives us every single time with grace that cleanses and restores.

Confession isn't about punishment; it's permission. Permission to stop carrying what you were never meant to hold. Permission to let go of guilt and walk in grace. Permission to be real with God so you can be whole with Him.

When you feel that internal nudge, after a harsh word, a selfish moment, a quiet compromise, don't ignore it; that's your invitation back to intimacy. The sooner you respond, the quicker healing flows. Grace is waiting.

When to Use This Prayer:

- When your heart feels heavy or distant from God
- After an argument, mistake, or emotional outburst
- When guilt or shame lingers longer than it should
- As part of your daily heart check-in with God

Try This: Whisper this simple prayer:

"God, I confess I [name the sin]. I receive Your full forgiveness. Help me walk in grace, not guilt." Let that moment of honesty be the first step into a fresh start.

Reflection Questions

1. Is there something you're carrying that God wants to lift off of you today?
2. What relationship in your life might need a moment of confession and reconnection?
3. How would your view of yourself shift if you truly received God's grace with open arms?

Confession is how we realign our hearts with God's. It's how we unclog the spiritual drains that keep us stuck. When we confess with sincerity and humility, chains fall, hearts soften, and we begin to walk lighter, freer. God doesn't just want to forgive you. He wants to renew you. You're still His. You're still loved. And He's not finished with your story.

For a deeper understanding of the impact of sin, consider the following passages:

1 John 3:4, 1 John 3:15, Matthew 5:22, Romans 1:32, and Ecclesi-astes. 7:29, Genesis 3:6, Romans 5:12-21, Matthew 5:19, Romans 3:23, James 1:13, 1 Peter 2:22, 1 Peter 5:8, 2 Samuel 24:1, 1 Chronicles 21:1, Acts 2:23, Psalm 119:160, James 2:10, Romans 8:7, Ephesians 2:1, Genesis 20:6, Acts 17:28, Romans 6:23, Mark 10:45, and Titus 2:14.

3. Intercession Prayer, When You're Called to Stand in the Gap

I urge, then, first of all, that petitions, prayers, intercession and thanksgiving be made for all people— for kings and all those in authority, that we may live peaceful and quiet lives in all godliness and holiness. — 1 Timothy 2:1–2, NIV.

Intercession is holy ground. It's what happens when love becomes prayer, when your heart breaks on behalf of someone else, and you bring their name before the throne of grace. It's not always loud. Often, it's whis-pered through tears, breathed in silence, or prayed while folding laundry or sitting in traffic. But heaven sees. And heaven moves.

Intercession is when you say, "Lord, be with them. Fight for them. Heal them. Cover them. Let them feel Your nearness." You're standing in the gap for someone else, not because you have the solution, but because you trust the One who does. Whether you're praying for a sick friend, a struggling child, or a nation in turmoil, intercession is how you partner with God in the spiritual realm. It's the ultimate act of love.

As a mom of seven, this is a daily rhythm for me. Whether I'm praying for their safety, wisdom, direction, or healing, I've come to realize interces-sion is one of the most powerful ways we show love. It's how we hold people close even when they're far away. It's how we cover them in the spirit even when we can't fix what's happening in the natural.

And it's not just for family or friends. Intercession widens the circle. It's for your church, your community, your leaders, and even for strangers you'll never meet but whose burdens God places on your heart. It's for the sick, the grieving, the lost, and the overwhelmed. When we intercede, we step into the spiritual realm and say, "God, I can't, but You can."

Jesus modeled this perfectly. He interceded for His disciples (John 17), for His enemies ("Father, forgive them…" Luke 23:34), and He continues to intercede for us right now (Romans 8:34, Hebrews 7:25). When we in-tercede, we echo His heart. We become vessels of His mercy, channels of His compassion, and messengers of His peace.

And here's the beautiful truth, you're not praying alone. Romans 8:26–27 reminds us that the Holy Spirit helps us in our weakness and intercedes for us with groanings too deep for words. So even when you don't know what to say, when your heart feels heavy and words fall short, the Spirit fills in the gaps.

In the same way the Spirit {comes to us and} helps us in our weakness. We do not know what prayer to offer or how to offer it as we should, but the Spirit Himself {knows our need and at the right time} intercedes on our behalf with sighs and groanings too deep for words. And He who searches the hearts knows what the mind of the Spirit is, because the Spirit intercedes {before God} on behalf of God's people in accordance with God's will. —Romans 8:26–27, AMP.

When to Use This Prayer

- When someone asks for prayer
- When someone unexpectedly comes to mind
- When you see a need you can't meet on your own
- When a situation is beyond human strength

Try This: Pause today and lift up one specific person. Speak their name out loud. Ask God to meet them, help them, and cover them with His love and strength. Even a whispered prayer becomes a powerful act of love in God's hands.

Reflection Questions

1. Who is God asking you to intercede for this week?
2. How might your prayers shift if you truly believed they were moving heaven?
3. Is there someone you've given up praying for that God is asking you to lift up again?

Intercession is not about having all the right words; it's about showing up with a willing heart. It's choosing love over apathy and faith over fear. Whether you cry, speak boldly, or sit in stillness, every act of intercession becomes a seed sown in the spirit. And God is faithful to bring the harvest.

So go ahead, stand in the gap. Pray the bold prayers. Whisper the desperate ones. Believe that your intercession is shaking chains, breaking barriers, and inviting heaven's help into earthly situations. Let your prayer be someone else's breakthrough.

For further study on Jesus as our intercessor, explore: Luke 22:32, John 17, Luke 23:34, Hebrews 7:25, Romans 8:26–27, and 1 Timothy 2:1.

4. Prayer of Thanksgiving, When Gratitude Becomes Your Weapon

Do not be anxious about anything, but in every situation, by prayer and petition, with thanksgiving, present your requests to God. — Philippians 4:6, NIV

Thanksgiving doesn't always change the circumstance, but it always transforms the soul.

Gratitude is more than good manners. It's a powerful, spiritual weapon that shifts our perspective from lack to abundance, from frustration to peace, from fear to faith, and from loneliness to an awareness of God's presence. It invites joy into weary places and turns our eyes away from what's wrong long enough to remember everything that's still right.

Some of my most powerful prayers didn't come in a moment of breakthrough, but in the middle of the mess, a whispered thanks for a warm breeze, a kind word, a soft hug from a child when I felt like I was unraveling. Gratitude anchored me. It pulled me back to the truth: God is still with me. God is still good.

A thankful heart doesn't ignore pain; it just chooses not to let pain have the final word. Gratitude reminds you that God has shown up before, and He'll show up again. That He's provided before, and He's not about to stop now. It becomes a lens of hope through which we view even our hardest seasons.

When you come to God in prayer, thanksgiving is how you begin to unlock peace; peace that surpasses understanding, peace that calms anxious thoughts, peace that anchors your spirit. Whether you're in a season of waiting, walking through grief, or simply feeling overwhelmed by the demands of everyday life, pausing to give thanks resets your heart and reopens the door to joy.

When we choose gratitude, especially in seasons that feel dry, disappointing, or confusing, we open the door to deeper faith, renewed joy, and the ability to endure with hope. Whether you're on a mountaintop or walking through a valley, let thanksgiving be your soundtrack. Let it be the way you end every prayer and begin every day. Even in uncertainty, there is always something to be grateful for.

When to Use This Prayer:

- When your heart feels heavy
- Before making a request
- When you feel anxious, discontent, or stuck
- When you need a perspective shift

Try This: List three things you're thankful for right now, big or small. Speak them out loud. Then begin your next prayer by saying, "God, thank You for…" and watch how your tone begins to shift.

Reflection Questions

1. What blessings have I overlooked today?
2. How might my prayers sound different if I started with thanks instead of requests?
3. What's one way I can make gratitude a daily habit, even on hard days?

Gratitude is how we steward joy. It's how we fight back against weariness and fear. It's not just the final line of a polite prayer, it's the very posture that unlocks heaven's peace. So when life feels heavy, uncertain, or even unfair, lift your eyes. Thank God not only for what He's done, but for who He is.

Let thanksgiving be your reset, your anthem, your quiet strength. Because **the woman who can still say "thank You" in the storm is the woman who is already walking in victory.**

For deeper study, explore: 1 Thessalonians 5:18, Ephesians 5:20, Colossians 3:17, Romans 7:25, Colossians 1:3–5, 1 Thessalonians 1:2–7; 2:13, Philippians 4:6, and Romans 8:28–29.

5. Petition Prayer, When You Need to Ask Boldly

Ask, and it will be given to you; seek, and you will find; knock, and the door will be opened to you. — Matthew 7:7, NIV

Let me remind you of something powerful: You are God's child, not a beggar.

Just like my kids know they can come to me when they need something, whether it's a snack, support, or simply a hug, you can come boldly to your Heavenly Father. He delights in you. And He delights in your asking.

A prayer of petition is when you bring your needs, desires, and concerns to God. Not with fear or shame, but with faith and expectation. You're not bothering Him. You're not asking for too much. You're simply doing what He's already invited you to do: Ask.

God longs for us to trust Him enough to come to Him first, before we vent, before we Google or Ask AI, and before we try to fix it all ourselves. He wants to be your first stop, not your last resort. There's a beautiful boldness in coming before God and saying, "Father, I need You."

Petition is not desperation; it's devotion. It's the prayer of a child who knows their Father listens. A woman who believes that heaven leans in when she speaks. A heart that has stopped pretending to be self-sufficient and has started walking in the confidence of divine dependence.

God never asked you to have it all together. He asked you to come. And in this beautiful act of prayer, you are invited to bring your needs, your wants, your hurts, your dreams...every detail. You're not an inconvenience. You're His beloved daughter. Your voice matters to Him. Your needs matter to Him.

I've whispered petition prayers in hospital rooms and parking lots. I've scribbled them in journals and shouted them from tear-stained pillows. *"God, please show me what to do." "God, I need Your peace." "Lord, we need provision, today."* And every time, He has shown Himself faithful. Not always in the way I imagined, but always in a way that reminded me He was present and He was still good. And I'm certain that it was always in a way that was best for me and my loved ones.

A prayer of petition doesn't require perfect words. It simply requires an open heart and a willingness to trust God with the outcome. You don't have to perform. You don't have to pretend. Just ask.

When to Use This Prayer:

- When you or your family have a specific need
- When you're unsure which direction to take
- When you need provision, healing, wisdom, or peace

Try This: Bring one personal need before God today. Be specific. Be honest. Say it out loud, write it down, or whisper it in prayer. Then, surrender the outcome with this reminder: *"God knows what I need, and He will provide in His perfect time."*

Reflection Questions

1. What's one thing you've been carrying alone that you haven't yet brought to God in prayer?
2. Have you confused asking boldly with asking selfishly?
3. How would your trust deepen if you believed that God delights in responding to your needs?

Asking boldly isn't arrogance; it's agreement. You're agreeing with God's Word that says He is your Provider. You're agreeing that He is good and generous. And you're aligning your heart with heaven's wisdom.

Petition is where faith meets honesty. It's the space where your vulnerability becomes a doorway to deeper intimacy with God. It's how we live out Philippians 4:6, bringing our requests not with anxiety, but with thanksgiving and expectation.

Do not be anxious or worried about anything, but in everything {every circumstance and situation} by prayer and petition with thanksgiving, continue to make your {specific} requests known to God. And the peace of God {that peace which reassures the heart, that peace} which transcends all understanding, {that peace which} stands guard over your hearts and your minds in Christ Jesus {is yours}.
—Philippians 4:6-7, AMP.

So go ahead, sis. Ask boldly. Knock persistently. Seek confidently. Whether you're praying for open doors, restored health, financial breakthrough, or simply clarity in the chaos, your prayers are not falling into silence. They're rising to the throne of grace.

For further study, spend time in: Psalm 37:4, Psalm 12:5, Psalm 69:33, Isaiah 58:11, Matthew 6:8, Matthew 14:16, Philippians 4:19, Hebrews 4:16, and 2 Peter 1:3.

6. Spiritual Warfare Prayer, When the Battle Isn't Just Natural

The weapons we fight with are not the weapons of the world. On the contrary, they have divine power to demolish strongholds. We demolish arguments and every pretension that sets itself up against the knowledge of God, and we take captive every thought to make it obedient to Christ. — 2 Corinthians 10:4–5, NIV

Some storms you can't explain. You're doing everything right, but everything feels wrong. The pressure is rising. Your thoughts are heavy. The atmosphere in your home feels off. You're tired...not just physically, but spiritually. That's when you know, this isn't just a natural fight. It's a spiritual one. And spiritual battles require spiritual weapons.

I've walked through seasons when everything felt like it was falling apart, not because I was doing something wrong, but because I was moving in the right direction. That's when I learned how to fight with the Word, with worship, and with unwavering prayer.

Spiritual warfare is real. But so is your authority in Christ (Matthew 9:8, Matthew 10:1, Matthew 16:19, Luke 10:19).

This isn't about spooky language or fear-driven living. This is about recognizing that we have a real enemy who would love to keep you distracted, discouraged, and defeated, but we serve a victorious Savior who has already overcome.

When peace feels unreachable and joy seems far away, you don't just need relief. You need resistance. And God has given you the weapons to resist every attack of the enemy. You don't have to guess your way through this fight. You've been equipped.

When to Use This Prayer

- When you feel spiritually attacked
- When fear, confusion, or chaos rises in your mind or home
- When you are contending for breakthrough in your family, marriage, health, or purpose

Your Battle Plan: From Ephesians 6:10–18

1. **Truth as your belt:** Stand firm in who God is and what He says.
2. **Righteousness as your breastplate:** Protect your heart with integrity and obedience.
3. **Peace on your feet:** Walk boldly, grounded in the gospel.
4. **Faith as your shield:** Guard your mind from lies and accusations.

5. **Salvation as your helmet:** Remember who you are and Whose you are.
6. **The Word as your sword:** Speak it. Declare it. Believe it.

The Armor of God

"In conclusion, be strong in the Lord [draw your strength from Him and be empowered through your union with Him] and in the power of His [boundless] might. Put on the full armor of God [for His precepts are like the splendid armor of a heavily-armed soldier], so that you may be able to [successfully] stand up against all the schemes and the strategies and the deceits of the devil. For our struggle is not against flesh and blood [contending only with physical opponents], but against the rulers, against the powers, against the world forces of this [present] darkness, against the spiritual forces of wickedness in the heavenly (supernatural) places. Therefore, put on the complete armor of God, so that you will be able to [successfully] resist and stand your ground in the evil day [of danger], and having done everything [that the crisis demands], to stand firm [in your place, fully prepared, immovable, victorious]. So stand firm and hold your ground, having tightened the wide band of truth (personal integrity, moral courage) around your waist and having put on the breastplate of righteousness (an upright heart), and having strapped on your feet the gospel of peace in preparation [to face the enemy with firm-footed stability and the readiness produced by the good news]. Above all, lift up the [protective] shield of faith with which you can extinguish all the flaming arrows of the evil one. And take the helmet of salvation, and the sword of the Spirit, which is the Word of God.

With all prayer and petition pray [with specific requests] at all times [on every occasion and in every season] in the Spirit, and with this in view, stay alert with all perseverance and petition [interceding in prayer] for all God's people." — Ephesians 6:10-18, AMP

You're not powerless. You're not fighting alone. And this is not the end of your story.

Try This: Declare God's Word out loud. Bind every scheme of the enemy in Jesus' name. Walk through your home, your child's room, or your workplace and speak life, truth, peace, and victory. Don't whisper, speak boldly with confidence. Warfare is meant to be loud when necessary. Let heaven (and hell) know whose side you're on.

Reflection

1. What lie is the enemy trying to get you to believe today?
2. What truth from God's Word do you need to speak louder?

In moments of intense pressure, don't shrink, stand. Even if all you can do is whisper, whisper in faith. Pray with grit. Worship when it hurts. Cry out with authority. And remember: You don't fight for victory, you fight from the position of it.

These are the moments that require prayer with power, not panic. This is when you lift your head, open your mouth, and declare God's Word back to every dark thing trying to intimidate, manipulate, or paralyze you.

This is spiritual warfare, and yes, you were born for it. Not because you're perfect. Not because you feel strong. But because the Spirit of the Living God dwells inside of you. He has given you everything you need to stand firm and push back the darkness, not just for yourself but for your family, your friendships, and your future.

You don't have to have all the answers, but you do have to know where your help comes from and be willing to use the spiritual weapons He's given you.

When the enemy tries to invade your territory, your peace, your marriage, your purpose, don't retreat. Rise up, armor up and pray. Because you are worth fighting for, and with God on your side, you will not lose.

For our struggle is not against flesh and blood {contending only with physical opponents}, but against the rulers, against the powers, against the world forces of this {present} darkness, against the spiritual forces of wickedness in the heavenly (supernatural) places. —Ephesians 6:12, AMP

For further study, dig into: Isaiah 54:17, Matthew 16:18, Ephesians 6:12, 2 Corinthians 10:4–5, Ephesians 6:10–18, 2 Timothy 1:7.

Chapter Wrap-Up: Your Complete Prayer Toolkit

You did more than read this chapter; you showed up for your life. You leaned into healing. You unpacked spiritual tools that will anchor you when the winds blow and strengthen you when your soul feels weary.

Prayer is not just something you do; it is a profound experience. It's who you're becoming.

You've now discovered how to worship through the overwhelm, confess your way back into alignment, stand in the gap for others, thank God in everything, ask with bold faith, and fight back when the enemy comes too close.

These are not just words on a page. These are spiritual weapons. Lifelines. Anchors. Keys. And now they're yours.

Let that sink in: You have a divine arsenal at your fingertips. You don't have to wonder if God hears you. You don't have to stay stuck in silence or confusion. You know how to move, how to cry out, press in, and pray through. You've been equipped.

And the best part? You don't have to get it perfect. You just have to be present. Faithful. Willing to meet God in the moments that feel messy, mundane, or miraculous. Every time you pray, you are choosing power over panic, relationship over routine, and breakthrough over burnout.

Your Empowered Challenge This Week:

Choose the prayer style you've struggled with most, the one that feels the most uncomfortable or unfamiliar. Maybe it's confession. Maybe it's warfare. Whatever it is, lean in. Practice it each day this week with bold intentionality. Watch how God meets you there. And don't forget to journal the revelations, nudges, or unexpected moments of peace that come.

What's Next:

Now that you've strengthened your voice in prayer, it's time to lean into something just as transformative, learning to hear God's voice for yourself.

In Chapter 5, you'll discover how to recognize when God is speaking, how He communicates through His Word, His whisper, and even your daily circumstances.

You're not just learning to pray.

You're learning to commune.

You're not just becoming a woman who talks to God,

You're becoming a woman who listens, discerns, and walks in divine rhythm. And that changes everything.

CHAPTER 5

Hearing God's Voice In Prayer

Hearing God: Learning to Recognize His Voice in Every Season

You've poured out your heart in prayer. You've worshiped, confessed, interceded, given thanks, asked boldly, and fought spiritually. But now comes the question every woman of faith eventually asks: "How do I know if God is speaking back?"

The truth is, He is. The problem isn't that God is silent. It's that life is loud. Between the noise of our schedules, the pressure of our responsibilities, and the endless voices of opinion, social media, and doubt, it can be hard to discern God's still, small voice. But it's there. Always. Whispering, guiding, reminding, reassuring. And you, my friend, were created to hear Him.

You don't need a title, a microphone, or a degree in theology. You need a tender heart and a listening posture. Because God doesn't just want to talk at you, He wants to walk with you. In every decision, every storm, every season.

In this chapter, we're going to break down the different ways God speaks through Scripture, through His Spirit, through other people, and even through the patterns and pauses of your life. You'll learn how to quiet the noise, tune your heart, and develop confidence in what you sense and hear. Because hearing God's voice doesn't just build your faith, it guides your future.

So take a breath. Lean in. God's not distant. He's not ignoring you. He's speaking right now. Let's learn how to listen.

Knowing the Sound of His Voice

One of the greatest joys of prayer is learning to recognize God's voice.

Over my 25 + years of marriage and raising seven children, I've learned that communication is key, not just in my home but also in my relationship with God. Just as my children know the sound of my voice, we can also learn to recognize when God is speaking to us. His voice will align with and echo His Word.

The Bible assures us, "My sheep hear My voice, and I know them, and they follow Me" (John 10:27, NKJV). God is always speaking; we just need to be aware of His presence and tune our hearts to listen to Him.

I'll never forget a moment I realized God was speaking to me. I was in the school pickup line, running on coffee and chaos after a sleepless night of worry about keeping up with life. My heart was heavy with decisions, questions, and quiet frustration. And then, like a whisper that cut through the noise of all the vehicles and children escaping from the school day, I sensed it: "Stop striving, beloved. I've got this."

It wasn't loud. It wasn't spooky. It was peaceful. Loving. Comforting. And it wasn't me, it was Him. That moment changed my prayer life forever. I stopped thinking of prayer as a one-way street and started embracing it as a conversation. Because prayer isn't just about you speaking to God, it's about learning to listen when He talks back.

And here's the truth that changed everything for me: God speaks to women like us. Not just to prophets or pastors. Not just to people with perfect spiritual résumés. He speaks to moms in carpool lanes, women in waiting seasons, tired hearts at midnight, and anyone who dares to believe He wants to be heard.

You Were Created to Hear Him

Jesus said, "My sheep hear My voice, and I know them, and they follow Me" (John 10:27, NKJV). That means if you belong to Him, you can hear Him. Period.

God has always spoken to ordinary people, mothers, teenagers, children, farmers and fishermen, and He still does today. But we often miss His voice, not because He's silent, but because our lives are noisy. Schedules, screens, self-doubt, and fear. All of it can crowd out His gentle whispers. But when we learn to quiet the noise, we can begin to hear the divine dialogue for which we were made.

Let's take this journey together to explore how God speaks, what gets in the way, how to tune our spiritual ears, and what to do when we're unsure we're hearing correctly. Because hearing God's voice isn't just possible, it's powerful.

How God Speaks: His Favorite Channels

Here are some of the most common ways God speaks to us:

1. Through Scripture

This is His primary voice. When a verse keeps showing up in your life, whether in your reading, on social media, or in conversation, pay attention. God is highlighting something for you.

All Scripture is God-breathed {given by divine inspiration} and is profitable for instruction, for conviction {of sin}, for correction {of error and restoration to obedience}, for training in righteousness {learning to live in conformity to God's will, both publicly and privately—behaving honorably with personal integrity and moral courage};
—2 Timothy 3:16, AMP.

2. Through the Holy Spirit

It might be a prompting, a nudge, or a peaceful knowing. He often speaks in stillness, not through shouts.

3. Through Godly People

Through mentors, pastors, and friends…God often uses others to confirm His message to you.

4. Through Circumstances

An open door, a closed one, divine timing, a redirection, He uses real life to guide us.

5. Through Dreams and Impressions

Though less common, God still speaks this way, especially when we're seeking direction or comfort.

But What If I'm Not Sure It's God?

If you've ever wondered, "Was that really God or just my own thoughts?" you're not alone. Here's how to test it:

1. Does it align with the Bible? God's voice never contradicts His Word.
2. Does it bring peace? God's voice is gentle, not fear-driven or condemning (Colossians 3:15).
3. Does it bear fruit? God's voice leads to growth, love, obedience, and truth (Matthew 7:16).

Is it confirmed by wise counsel? God often uses others to affirm and confirm His leading (Proverbs 15:22).

When Life Is Loud, Create Space

The reason we don't hear God isn't usually spiritual failure; it's spiritual busyness. You may need to do what I've had to do again and again: Make room. Slow down. Be still.

Try this:

- After praying, say: "God, I'm listening. What do You want to say to me?"
- Then sit quietly for a few minutes.
- Write anything you sense in a journal, words, scriptures, images, or emotions.

Even in your busy life, God is speaking. While folding laundry, driving, cooking, or walking. He doesn't need a perfect sanctuary to show up, He just needs your invitation.

Common Blocks to Hearing God

1. *"I don't hear anything."*: That's okay. Silence doesn't mean absence. Sometimes God is preparing your heart or teaching you to wait.
2. *"I'm afraid I'll get it wrong."*: That fear is valid, but God's grace is bigger. He'll gently redirect you if needed.

3. *"I can't tell if it's me or God."*: Start journaling and looking for patterns. God's voice sounds like peace, clarity, and love.
4. *"I don't feel worthy."*: Friend, worth has nothing to do with it. He loves you, and your willingness and faith is enough.

Build a Lifestyle of Listening

You don't need hours of quiet time to hear from God. You need a habit of listening:

- Morning: "God, what do You want me to know today?"
- Evening: "God, where did I see You today?"
- During chores: "God, speak to me as I serve."
- While driving: Turn worship music on and let your heart tune in.

Real Life Example:

A few years ago, I was unsure whether to pursue a big opportunity in my coaching business. I prayed, but felt torn. One day during a walk, I quietly asked, "Lord, is this You or just me?" And in that moment, I saw a mom and daughter holding hands and laughing. It felt like God whispering, "Your first ministry is home." I knew what to do. Seasons of life change, but there are some seasons and experiences you can't get back once they're gone. I was at peace and that was an indication of God's presence and answer. His voice brings freedom, not fear.

Reflection Questions:

1. When was a time you think God may have spoken to you?
2. What keeps you from slowing down and listening for His voice?
3. What practice will you commit to this week to create space for God to speak?

Practical Exercise: Your 7-Day Listening Challenge

Day 1: Spend 5 minutes in silence after prayer, asking God to speak to you about His love for you.

Day 2: Ask God to highlight one scripture verse for you during your Bible reading. Write it down and think about it throughout the day.

Day 3: During a routine task, ask God: "What do You want me to know about this situation I'm facing?"

Day 4: Listen for God's voice about someone you need to pray for or encourage.

Day 5: Ask God to show you one way He's been faithful in your life this week.

Day 6: Bring a decision you're facing to God and listen for His guidance.

Day 7: Simply ask: "God, what's on Your heart for me today?"

A Prayer to Hear His Voice

Heavenly Father,

Thank You for being a God who speaks. Thank You that I don't have to earn Your voice, I simply have to listen. Help me quiet the noise, calm the chaos, and create sacred space in my life to hear You. Teach me to recognize Your whispers in the middle of my routines, my challenges, and my waiting seasons. Let Your Word be the loudest voice in my heart. When I feel unsure, bring peace. When I doubt, bring clarity. And when I hear You, give me the courage to follow. I'm listening, Lord. Speak to me.

In Jesus' Name, Amen.

Next Up: Now that you're learning to hear from God, it's time to capture what He says. In Chapter 6, we'll explore how journaling your prayers creates a record of His faithfulness and a legacy of intimacy with the One who loves you most.

Journaling as a Tool for Spiritual Growth

Writing Your Way Closer to God

Over the years, as I've raised a family, I've learned that time flies. From endless diaper changes, school drop-offs, sporting events, bedtime stories, and about a million *"Mom, where's my...?"* moments. One minute, you're rocking a newborn at 2 AM, and the next, you're watching that same baby drive off in your car! In the blur of it all, it's easy to miss the small, beautiful ways God is working. Yet He's there in every messy, joyful, chaotic moment.

Life moves so quickly at times that, deep down, I know I need to ask myself way more often, *"Have I paused long enough to hear God's voice?"*. Between making breakfast, refereeing sibling arguments, and catching up on emails, I try to pray, but I don't always know how well I'm doing at listening. Have I captured anything God whispers back after I pray?

That realization launched me into one of the most life-giving habits I've ever embraced: journaling my prayers. What began as a simple notebook on my nightstand became a sacred space where I could meet God in honesty, reflection, and intimacy. Journaling helped me recognize His voice in the everyday journey, remember His hand in past seasons, and trust Him more deeply in the present. And friend, it can do the same for you.

Life as a mom, a woman, a wife, a daughter, and a dreamer: it truly moves fast. Scratch that. It sprints. We juggle so much, from laundry piles and carpool lines to deadlines, work days, doctor visits, grocery lists, dinner plans, community service, ministry, and the emotions of everyone in the house. We're often so busy managing life that we forget to process it. We survive days without fully remembering what God did in them. That's where journaling becomes more than just a spiritual suggestion; it becomes a lifeline.

Journaling Slows Us Down and Builds Us Up

In a world that pushes us to scroll and swipe, journaling invites us to pause and reflect. It's a personal sanctuary where your thoughts, prayers, fears, and victories find a home. It doesn't have to be poetic. It doesn't have to be polished. It just has to be honest. And the more honest you are, the more powerful it becomes.

A prayer journal is more than a diary; it's a spiritual receipt book. A record of God's goodness, His whispers, His miracles in the middle of your mess. It's how we anchor our faith when the storms come and how we pass on a legacy of trust to the generations behind us.

Why Journaling Enhances Your Prayer Life

Let me say this upfront: You don't need a fancy pen or leather-bound notebook to encounter God through journaling. What you need is a willing heart, a few minutes of quiet, and the courage to show up with your whole self: tired, hopeful, uncertain, joyful, or somewhere in between.

Here's why journaling is a game-changer for your spiritual life:

1. It Makes Your Prayers More Intentional and Specific

Before I started journaling, my prayers were often vague and lacked direction. "Lord, bless my family." "Help me today." There's nothing wrong with those, but writing down my prayers helped me focus and be specific. It reminded me that God is not just the God of the big picture; He's also the God of the little details.

Instead of "Help my child," I'd write: "Lord, give my son _____ peace today as he takes that test. Calm his nerves and remind him that You're with him in that classroom." That's the beauty of written prayer. It slows you down just enough to dig deeper.

2. It Builds Your Faith as You Record Answered Prayers

There's nothing quite like flipping through your journal and seeing the fingerprints of God all over your life. Prayers you wrote in tears that were answered with joy. Concerns that felt overwhelming, now resolved in His perfect timing. Doors that shut, only to see better ones swing wide open.

One entry from three years ago still brings tears to my eyes. I wrote, "Lord, I have no idea how we're going to afford this school tuition, but I trust You." At the time, we were financially stretched, and I was anxious. Months later, my son received an unexpected scholarship from the school itself. That journal entry is now circled with a big "GOD DID IT!". I wouldn't remember all those details if I hadn't written them down.

That's what journaling does. It captures miracles and prayers answered, both big and small, in real-time, so that you can revisit them in the wilderness or during more challenging times.

Those who sow in tears Shall reap in joy. —Psalm 126:5, NKJV

3. It Helps You Recognize God's Voice and Patterns

As you write your prayers, scriptures, and reflections, you'll begin to notice themes and patterns. Certain verses will keep showing up. Certain words or impressions will return. Over time, you'll become more confident in recognizing how God speaks uniquely to you.

He may speak through peace that overrides panic, through a scripture that shows up three different ways in one week, or through a quiet knowing in your spirit. Journaling makes these moments stand out like highlighted notes from heaven.

How to Use Your Prayer Journal Effectively

Your *Enhancing Your Journey: 90-Day Prayer Journal* (available on Amazon) is more than a pretty notebook; it's your spiritual growth partner. Here's how to use it in a way that's life-giving and sustainable:

Prayer Requests & Concerns

Write the date and the details. Be real. Be honest. Pray big.

Example Entry: April 5 – *Lord, I'm tired. I've been short-tempered with the kids, and I feel like I'm running on fumes. Please give me patience, grace, and rest today. Also, I am praying for wisdom about Maya's school situation. Should we keep her in this program or switch to a different one next year?*

Casting all your cares {all your anxieties, all your worries, and all your concerns, once and for all} on Him, for He cares about you {with deepest affection, and watches over you very carefully}. —*1 Peter 5:7, AMP.*

Scripture & Spiritual Insights

Write verses that stand out, along with what God seems to be saying through them.

Example Entry: *April 6 – Psalm 46:10: "Be still and know that I am God." I've seen this verse three times today. I feel like God is gently telling me to stop striving and trust that He's already working behind the scenes.*

For the word of God is living and active and full of power {making it operative, energizing, and effective}... —*Hebrews 4:12, AMP.*

Answered Prayers & God's Faithfulness

Use this space to write how God responded. Whether the answer was "yes," "wait," or even "no." Remember, even a "no" from God is never rejection; it's redirection. It's His loving protection, His perfect wisdom, and His way of guiding you toward something greater than what you could see in the moment.

What feels like a closed door today may later reveal itself as a divine detour to something better. Trust that He sees the whole picture, even when you only have a piece of the puzzle. This section becomes your personal evidence that God is always working faithfully, intentionally, and for your good.

Example Entry: April 20 – *Maya told me today she doesn't want to go back to her school next year. She's been praying too! We discussed it, and there's a new school we're considering that better suits her needs. Thank You, God, for confirming what we both sensed.*

I will {solemnly} remember the deeds of the Lord; Yes, I will {wholeheartedly} remember Your wonders of old. —*Psalm 77:11, AMP*

Daily Gratitude & God Sightings

Three things you're thankful for + any little moments where you saw God at work.

Example Entry: *April 25 – Grateful for 1) a surprise coffee drop-off from my friend, 2) no traffic this morning, and 3) laughter at dinner.*

Enter His gates with a song of thanksgiving, And His courts with praise. Be thankful to Him, bless and praise His name. —Psalm 100:4, AMP

God sighting: My son came up and hugged me out of nowhere and said, "You're doing a good job, Mom." That was You, Lord.

In every situation {no matter what the circumstances} be thankful and continually give thanks to God; for this is the will of God for you in Christ Jesus.
—1 Thessalonians 5:18, AMP

Making Journaling Fit Your Season

1. **For the Early Bird**: Start your day with a quiet moment and a cup of coffee. Even five minutes can ground your entire day in gratitude and clarity.
2. **For the Night Owl**: Wind down with your journal before bed. Write what went well, what you're surrendering, and how you saw God move.
3. **For the Constantly Interrupted Woman**: Keep your journal in the car, kitchen, or purse. Jot quick thoughts during nap time, carpool, on a lunch break, or even in the bathroom (no shame!).
4. **For the Perfectionist**: Your journal doesn't need to be "pretty." Bullet points, scribbles, stick figures, or even emojis. If it helps you process and pray, it counts.

When Life Feels Overwhelming

On the hard days, try this simple approach:

List Prayers:
* Energy to get through today

- Peace for the argument with my husband
- Guidance to parent my teen
- Wisdom about the new job
- Strength to forgive
- Thankful for leftovers, not having to cook, and hugs

Letters to God:

Dear God,

I'm confused and tired. I know You're good, but I'm struggling to see it right now. Please remind me that You're with me. Help me not to give up...

Final Encouragement

Your journal will become a treasure chest of transformation. One day, you'll look back at these pages and see the fingerprints of God all over your life. The struggles you thought would break you, the prayers you didn't think He heard, the quiet miracles that slowly unfolded. These aren't just notes on a page; they are proof that your faith is alive, your prayers matter, and your God is near.

Your journal is a testimony in the making. One day, you will look back at these pages and see the hand of God woven into your life story. The problems that once seemed insurmountable will be victories written in ink. The prayers that felt like whispers will be shouts of praise as you see God's faithfulness unfold.

So, grab your journal, open your heart, and start writing. Create a legacy of faith for the generations watching you walk with Him. Your journey of faith is worth recording!

Reflection Questions:

1. What's been holding you back from journaling consistently?
2. How has God shown up for you lately, even in small ways?
3. What prayer or promise do you want to record and believe for today?

Prayer for Your Journaling Journey

Lord,

Thank You for meeting me in the pages of my story. Help me to pause, reflect, and listen. Teach me to capture Your goodness, to write down Your whispers, and to treasure the journey we're on together. Let my journal become a place where faith grows, healing begins, and testimony is recorded. I trust that every page will show more of You and less of me. Help me begin; even if it's messy, even if it's brief. I'm ready.

In Jesus' Name, Amen.

CHAPTER 7

Establishing a Daily Prayer Routine

The Steady Prayer Rhythm: Building a Prayer Life That Transforms Your Everyday Chaos

It was 6:47 AM when my teenage son walked into the kitchen, obviously angry and frustrated because his favorite basketball shirt was in the laundry. My youngest was crying because one of her older brothers was torturing her, my husband was frantically searching for the car keys, and I was standing there in my pajamas, holding a cold cup of coffee, wondering how the morning had already spiraled out of control.

Sound familiar?

In that moment, I did what many of us do: I sent up a desperate, silent plea. "God, help me get through this day." But as I rushed to find another shirt for my son, prep breakfast, and help find those keys, I realized something that changed my outlook: What if prayer wasn't just my emergency hotline to heaven? What if it could be the steady rhythm all day long that actually prevented some of this beautiful chaos from overwhelming me?

That morning marked the beginning of my journey toward what I now call a "**steady prayer rhythm**", a daily lifeline that anchors me through the highs and lows of being a woman and through this motherhood journey. And sis, if you're reading this while hiding in your car after drop-off, during a lunch break, or during those precious few minutes before your family wakes up, I want you to know: You don't need another thing on your to-do list. You need a lifeline. Prayer can be exactly that.

Prayer isn't meant to be an occasional emergency call; it's meant to be the rhythm of our daily lives. Prayer is also not meant to be used only at a time of pressure. It's meant to be a continual place of refuge. A strong, consistent prayer routine invites ongoing intimacy with God, deepens our faith, and establishes a foundation that helps us navigate life's challenges. It doesn't demand perfection or performance; it simply asks us to show up. God is not looking for a perfect routine. He's looking for an open heart.

Let me show you how to create this sacred rhythm in a way that works for your life.

Start by setting aside dedicated time for prayer. Jesus Himself modeled this when He withdrew to a solitary place early in the morning to pray (Mark 1:35 NIV). If mornings work for you, wonderful. If not, don't worry; God is always available, 24/7. The key is consistency. Treat it like an appointment with God because it is. Even 5–10 minutes a day can create a powerful habit that roots your heart in His presence. Finding time to pray isn't always easy, but don't underestimate the impact of this daily connection. It helps us walk in power, authority, boldness, and love.

Next, create a prayer space. It doesn't need to be elaborate, just a quiet place where you can meet with God. Keep a Bible, journal, and pen nearby. Add a candle or soft worship music to create a serene atmosphere. Remove distractions and create an environment that allows your heart to settle. A clutter-free corner or a simple nook can become holy ground when you meet God there.

Of course, even with the best of intentions, distractions will come. That's why it's important to develop a strategy for overcoming them. Put your phone on "Do Not Disturb." Start with worship. Psalm 100:4 reminds us to enter His gates with thanksgiving and His courts with praise. Praise helps shift your perspective. Pray out loud if it helps you stay awake or focused. Or write your prayers in a journal to anchor your thoughts. Documenting what you're asking for and how God answers not only builds faith but also becomes a spiritual legacy.

Above all, be consistent. Relationships grow with time and effort. Imagine if I spoke to my husband only once a month or checked in with my kids only when they were in need of help. Our relationships would suffer. The same applies to our relationship with God. Draw near to Him, and He will draw near to you (James 4:8).

A simple way to stay consistent is by tying prayer to daily habits. Pray while your coffee brews. Talk to God on your commute. Whisper a prayer during bedtime routines. You can also join a prayer group or find an accountability partner. Community creates encouragement.

I've also developed a simple, flexible method for prayer for busy women and moms called **the GRACE Method:**

G: Gather Yourself in God's Presence
R: Reflect on His Faithfulness
A: Ask with Confidence
C: Converse Honestly
E: Extend Gratitude

Whether you have five minutes or fifty, this framework creates space to invite God in. This isn't a formula; it's just a flexible framework designed to meet you wherever you are in your day.

Start by gathering yourself in God's presence. Before rushing into your to-do list or unloading your worries, pause to acknowledge Him. It can be as simple as taking a deep breath, whispering His name, or looking out your window and noticing something beautiful. Even 90 seconds while the coffee brews can become sacred when your heart is focused.

Next, reflect on His faithfulness. Look back on the ways He's shown up for you, big and small. The answered prayers, the unexpected provisions, the peace that came when it shouldn't have. Remembering how He moved in the past builds faith for what you're facing now.

Then ask boldly. Bring your honest, raw, and everyday needs to Him. Ask for strength when you're tired, peace when you're anxious, wisdom when you're unsure, and grace when you've had enough. Nothing is too small or too messy for Him.

Then, converse honestly. Prayer isn't a monologue; it's a conversation. Be real about your joys, your disappointments, your fears, and even your frustrations. God can handle it all. He isn't intimidated by your emotions. He welcomes them.

Finally, extend gratitude. Even in the mess. Even when you're still waiting. Thank Him for breath in your lungs, food on the table, or a child's unexpected hug. Gratitude shifts our perspective and helps us see His presence in the everyday.

You don't need a perfect prayer closet to do this. A coffee corner, your car, the bathroom, the closet, or a corner of your bedroom can all become sacred space. The key is to remove distractions and show up. Some days will be interrupted. Some days will be quiet and rich in meaning. Others will be rushed and scattered. It's all okay. Grace covers your efforts.

I know distractions are real. The laundry, the notifications, the never-ending mental checklist. But minor adjustments can help. Remember, attach prayer to existing habits: while brushing your teeth, during your commute, or as you drink your morning coffee. If you need help staying consistent, consider joining a prayer group or finding a prayer partner to support you.

Some women thrive with structure. If that's you, try assigning themes to each day: Monday for your marriage, Tuesday is for your children, Wednesday for wisdom, Thursday for gratitude, Friday for friends and extended family, Saturday for service and calling, and Sunday for surrender. We each have different relationships and situations that are important or of concern to us so choose what themes apply to you in this current season of your life. However, spreading your focus allows you to pray with intention without feeling overwhelmed.

The more you prioritize this sacred rhythm, the more you'll notice its fruit. I became more patient, more present, and more at peace. My children began to mirror what they saw: my daughter asked me to pray with her before school, and my son began whispering his own bedtime prayers. My home has become a sanctuary, not because of its décor or quietness, but because we acknowledge and welcome God's presence there regularly.

Dear Sister

Sis, your steady prayer rhythm doesn't need to look like anyone else's. It simply needs to reflect your heart's desire to walk with God. Whether it's five minutes before the house wakes up, a whispered prayer in the carpool lane, or a bedtime conversation with Jesus, it all matters. The goal is not perfection. The goal is presence. Let prayer become the beat that steadies your soul and anchors your day.

> *Come to Me, all you who labor and are heavy laden, and I will give you rest.*
> —*Matthew 11:28, NKJV.*

He's waiting for you, just as you are, right where you are. Let your steady prayer rhythm with Him begin now.

In your prayer rhytm don't forget to talk about your victories, and record your answered prayers. In your prayer journal, create a section called "Answered Prayers & God's Faithfulness." Write how God responded, even if the answer was "wait" or "no," that led to something better.

Remember, God's "no" is never rejection; it's often His redirection. He sees what we can't. These moments reveal His wisdom, protection, and provision. When the answer is no, it's highly likely that something or someone better is coming. Keep going and run on to see what the end is going to be.

And record all of that too.

His timing is always rooted in love. Reflecting on God's answers, especially in seasons of doubt, reminds you that He is faithful and that His plans are worth trusting.

So here's your gentle challenge: Choose one part of your day, morning, noon, or night, and dedicate just five minutes to prayer using this GRACE method. Keep it simple, keep it honest, and watch how even a small daily habit can begin to transform everything.

Chapter Wrap-Up: Your Sacred Rhythm Is Just Beginning

Pray without ceasing, —1 *Thessalonians* 5:17, *NKJV*

By now, you've probably realized something beautifully unexpected: prayer is less about performance and more about presence. Less about lofty words and more about intentional moments. And friend, you don't need to be a perfect woman to be a praying one. You just need to be willing.

This chapter gave you more than a to-do list. It provided you with tools for healing, space for connection, and a gentle invitation to build a life grounded in steady prayer rhythm.

From that first whispered "God, I need You" to the messy, grace-filled journaling during nap time or your tea or coffee break, every moment of prayer matters. Every breath lifted toward heaven counts. You've been equipped to build a prayer life that feels less like pressure and more like peace. That's the power of spiritual consistency.

This isn't just about talking to God, it's about walking with Him. So every now and then, check in with yourself and ask, *"Am I still walking with Him?"* When you acknowledge He is always walking with or carrying you, you can gather yourself in His presence. When you reflect on His faithfulness, ask boldly, converse honestly, and extend gratitude, you don't just survive the day; you grow through it. You lead your home with wisdom. You love your family with endurance. And you overcome with hope. You're not just learning how to pray, you're becoming a praying woman. And that changes everything.

Reflection Questions:

1. What time of day feels most natural for me to connect with God?
2. And how can I protect that time?

3. What distractions often prevent me from praying, and how can I overcome them?
4. How has God answered my prayers in the past?
5. What area of my life needs more consistent prayer?
6. What would it look like to invite God into the small moments of my day?

Prayer for a Steady Prayer Rhythm:

Heavenly Father,

Thank You for desiring a relationship with me that is real, ongoing, and deeply personal. Teach me how to meet with You daily, not out of obligation, but out of love. Help me create rhythms that are sustainable in this season of life. When I'm overwhelmed, draw me close. When I'm distracted, gently redirect me. May prayer become as natural as breathing, and my first response, not my last resort. Thank You for being with me, always listening, and lovingly guiding me.

In Jesus' Name, Amen.

CHAPTER 8

Scripture and Prayer – How to Pray God's Word

When Words Won't Come: Praying God's Word Back to Him

There are moments in womanhood and in life, when the weight is just too heavy, and words feel impossible. I've had nights where I sat in the darkness, heart aching, tears flowing, and nothing would come out. The grief and heartbreak I was facing were so great that I didn't know how to pray. I didn't have the energy or the eloquence.

Maybe you've been there too, those 2 AM hours when the pain is raw, when you're too exhausted to form complete sentences, let alone full prayers. And yet, there is hope. Because in those moments, God meets us with a lifeline: His Word.

When our words run dry, His Word speaks loud and clear, and the Holy Spirit can help us and make intercession for us in our weakness (Romans 8:26, NKJV). The Bible is not just a book of ancient history; it's a living, breathing manual for real-life prayer. It's God's gift to us for the moments when we're broken, burdened, or simply blank. Hebrews 4:12 reminds us that His Word is alive and active. It doesn't just sit on a shelf; it shapes our hearts, anchors our emotions, and realigns our perspectives when life feels upside down.

Praying Scripture isn't about getting the words perfect. It's about coming into agreement with heaven. When we pray God's promises back to Him, we aren't just hoping He hears us; we are standing on truth, wielding our spiritual sword, and activating divine authority over our homes, hearts, and situations. Imagine the confidence that comes when you stop wondering what to say and start declaring what God has already said.

I remember kneeling beside one of my children's beds one night after something had occurred that broke my heart, an incident that I knew could be harmful to their life and future. I had nothing left. So I opened my Bible and began to whisper God's promises aloud. What I couldn't say in my own words, I borrowed from His.

In that holy exchange, my burden lifted, and my peace returned. His Word became my words, and it transformed my entire mindset about the matter, restoring hope that this is not the end of the story. If you are facing anything similar that is a shock to your system or family, this is not the end of your story either.

My friend Denise experienced something similar. Her home was under siege, her marriage was crumbling, her finances were in ruins, and her teenage son was spiraling. She felt helpless until she began her own "Scripture Prayer Challenge."

Each day for 30 days, she chose one verse and prayed it over her family. She'd write the verse on a sticky note, place it on her bathroom mirror or coffee pot, and pray it every time she passed by. She didn't always feel different, but she kept at it. And by the end of the 30 days, the atmosphere in her home had shifted. Her husband found work. Her son started turning around. Her heart felt steady. Not because her words were magical, but because God's Word never fails (see Isaiah 55:11, Ezekiel 12:25).

God is not a man, that He should lie, Nor a son of man, that He should repent. Has He said, and will He not do? Or has He spoken, and will He not make it good?"
—Numbers 23:19, NKJV

That's the power of praying Scripture. You're not begging God, you're aligning with Him. You're reminding yourself what's true, even when everything around you screams otherwise. You're not coming empty-handed, you're coming with the most powerful language in existence: the Word of God.

So will My word be which goes out of My mouth; It will not return to Me void (useless, without result), Without accomplishing what I desire, And without succeeding in the matter for which I sent it.. —Isaiah 55:11, AMP

So how do you start?

Try the S.P.E.A.K. Method:

S: Select a Scripture: Choose one verse that speaks to what you're walking through today.

P: Personalize It: Replace general language with your name, your loved one's name, or your child's name. Make it yours.

E: Expand the Prayer: Let that verse become a springboard. Talk to God about it. Be honest.

A: Ask for Application: Invite the Holy Spirit to show you how to live out that truth today.

K: Keep a Record: Write it down. Keep a prayer journal. Look back later and see what God did.

To help you begin, here are some Scripture-based prayers for everyday struggles:

1. **For exhaustion:** "Come to me, all you who are weary and burdened, and I will give you rest." (Matthew 11:28, NIV). Lord, my heart and body are worn thin. Wrap me in Your rest. Help me breathe again.

2. **For parenting challenges:** "Train up a child in the way he should go [teaching him to seek God's wisdom and will for his abilities and talents], Even when he is old he will not depart from it." (Proverbs 22:6, AMP). Father, help me see my child the way You do. Give me wisdom and grace to raise them well.

3. **For financial stress:** "And my God will liberally supply (fill until full) your every need according to His riches in glory in Christ Jesus." (Philippians 4:19, AMP). Jehovah Jireh, I trust You to provide for me. I place every bill, every known and unknown concern or problem, and every worry into Your hands.

4. **For peace:** "You will keep in perfect and constant peace the one whose mind is steadfast [that is, committed and focused on You—in both inclination and character], Because he trusts and takes refuge in You [with hope and confident expectation]." (Isaiah 26:3, AMP). God, center my mind. Guard my heart. Silence the noise and let Your peace reign.

5. **For guidance:** "Your word is a lamp to my feet and a light to my path." (Psalm 119:105, NKJV). Lead me, Lord. I don't know what's next, but I trust that You do. In Jesus' Name, amen.

Ready to build the habit? Here's your 7-Day Scripture Prayer Challenge:

- Choose one verse that speaks to your current struggle.
- Write it down and place it where you'll see it often.
- Pray it morning, noon, and night.
- Add your family's names into the verse.
- Find two more verses that support the theme.
- Declare those verses out loud.
- Reflect and journal on what you sense God doing.

As Scripture becomes the language of your prayers, you'll notice something beautiful: God's voice will become clearer, your prayers more confident, and your heart more anchored. Instead of scrambling for words in chaos, truth will rise up from within you.

Friend, when you don't know what to say, you're not weak, you're ready. You're ready to lean not on your own understanding, but on the living, breathing Word of God that never fails. He has already equipped you with everything you need. Now it's time to open your Bible, speak it out, and watch what He does.

Let His Word be the soundtrack of your life. Let it shape the atmosphere of your home. Let it be the bridge when your own words fall short. Because you, beloved, are not alone. And the God who wrote every line in that Book? He's listening. And He's responding.

This week's prayer point: Lord, give me a hunger for Your Word and a habit of praying it. Let Your promises take root in my heart and flow out of my mouth, especially when life leaves me speechless.

This week's challenge: Pray Psalm 91:1-2 every morning over your home. Speak it, believe it, and watch your atmosphere shift.

You don't have to be perfect. You just have to be present and willing to pray His Word back to Him. That's where the power is. That's where the peace begins.

Prayer Journal Prompts:

Use these in your quiet time this week to deepen your Scripture-based prayer journey.

1. Lord, the Scripture I feel most drawn to right now is: _____. I believe You are using it to speak to me about: _____.
2. When I pray this verse over my life, I'm asking You to help me trust You in the area of: _____.
3. I am currently believing God to fulfill this promise from His Word: _____.
4. One moment in my life where I clearly saw Scripture come alive was: _____.
5. A verse I want to teach my children (or the community I serve) this week is: _____ because I believe it will encourage them in: _____.

Reflection Questions:

1. What's one Bible verse you turn to when you feel overwhelmed or anxious? Why do you think it comforts you?
2. Have you ever seen God answer a prayer you prayed using Scripture? What did that experience teach you?
3. Are there any areas in your life where you've been praying your own words but need to shift to praying God's Word instead?
4. What fears, burdens, or situations in your life do you need to surrender into God's hands by praying His promises over them?
5. How can you make praying Scripture a habit in your daily routine, even in the busiest seasons of life?

A Powerful Prayer:

Father God,

Thank You for the gift of Your Word. Thank You that when my heart is weary and my lips feel silent, You've already given me the language of heaven to speak life into every situation. Teach me to love Scripture, not just as something to read but as something to live, speak, and pray. Let Your Word dwell richly in my heart. Help me raise my children or teach my community to have Your promises on their lips. Make my home a place where truth is declared boldly, and peace reigns deeply. When I don't know what to say, remind me that I don't need to have perfect words, just a willing heart. Let Your promises be my guide, Your truth be my weapon, and Your voice be

the one I trust above all.
    In Jesus' Name, Amen.

CHAPTER 9

When Prayers Seem Unanswered

Trusting God's Heart When You Can't Trace His Hand

It was just after bedtime when my daughter, in her sweetest voice, asked for ice cream. We had already brushed our teeth, put on our pajamas, and said our prayers. She knew the answer would be no, but she asked anyway, smiling, hopeful, and maybe a little manipulative. I looked at her lovingly and replied, "Not tonight, princess. I know you want it now, but your tummy and your teeth need rest more than sugar."

She frowned, disappointed. I kissed her forehead. She didn't understand, but I knew I was doing what was best for her. And isn't that how it feels sometimes with God?

We ask sometimes with tears in our eyes, sometimes with fierce faith, for what seems reasonable, good, and necessary: healing, breakthrough, a job, a spouse, reconciliation, direction, or relief. We ask with faith. We plead. And when the answer doesn't come quickly, or the silence stretches on, our hearts ache with questions: Did God hear me? Did I do something wrong? Is He even listening?

But here is the truth I've had to learn again and again: God's silence is not His absence. And a "not yet" is not the same as "no."

Even in my humanity as a mother, I know how to say "no" or "wait" when my children ask for something that would harm them or come at the wrong time. If they ask for dessert ten minutes before dinner, it's a "no". If they want the car keys before they've learned to drive, it's a definite "not yet". But when they ask for wisdom, strength, or comfort? I say yes, every time.

God answers us much the same way. Sometimes His answer is "Yes," and we rejoice. Sometimes it's "Wait," because He's orchestrating something behind the scenes. And sometimes it's "No," because He sees the whole picture we cannot.

I've lived through difficult seasons, times of deep hurt, betrayal, and loss. And rarely have I understood why in the middle of it all. But with time, I've come to know this: I can trust God's character even when I don't understand His choices. He is always good. Always wise. Always working for my good, even when I can't see it (Jeremiah 24:6, 29:11, 32:41).

When God's "No" Is Really Love in Disguise

Just like I withheld ice cream to protect my daughter, God sometimes withholds what we ask for, not to punish us, but to preserve us.

We want the open door. God sees the fire behind it. We want the relationship. God knows it would wreck our life and peace. We want the opportunity. God knows it would damage our confidence.

Isaiah 55:8-9 reminds us, "For my thoughts are not your thoughts, neither are your ways my ways... As the heavens are higher than the earth, so are my ways higher than your ways."

Unanswered prayers often mean that God is writing a better story than we imagined.

Key Principles to Remember When Facing Unanswered Prayers:

- God hears every prayer. Silence doesn't mean He's ignoring you.
- Check your motives. Are your desires aligned with His will? (James 4:3)
- Stay rooted in Scripture. His Word provides clarity and peace.
- Trust His timing. God is never late.
- Persevere in prayer. Faith is often proven through persistence. (Luke 18:1)
- Give thanks. Gratitude shifts our perspective (Philippians 4:6-7).
- Lean on community. Invite others to join you in believing and praying.

What to Do While You Wait

Waiting seasons can feel like wandering. They test our patience and faith. But they don't have to be wasted.

1. **Worship Anyway**: Worship shifts your focus from the problem to the Provider. Even when you feel discouraged, worship reminds your soul of God's worthiness (Psalm 34:1).
2. **Write It Down**: Journaling your prayers and reflections helps you trace God's hand over time (Habakkuk 2:2).
3. **Encourage Someone Else**: Sometimes God brings your break-through while you're blessing someone else (1 Thessalonians 5:11, Hebrews 10:24-25).
4. **Stay in the Word**: Combat lies with truth. Let Scripture speak louder than fear (2 Corinthians 10:5).
5. **Remember His Faithfulness**: Look back at what He's already done. Let it fuel your faith for what He'll do next (Hebrews 10:23).

Testimonies from the Waiting Room

Melanie's Story: Melanie prayed for years for her husband to come to Christ. She often felt alone in her faith and questioned whether God would ever move in his heart. One day, after nearly a decade of seemingly unanswered prayers, her husband came home from a men's retreat in tears, completely surrendered. She said, "All those years, God was working in the soil. I just couldn't see the roots growing beneath the surface."

Jasmine's Story: Jasmine battled infertility for seven years. Friends celebrated baby showers while she grieved silently. But she clung to the promise in Psalm 113:9, "He settles the childless woman in her home as a happy mother of children." Today, she's raising twin girls and calls them her "double portion."

You may be in your own waiting room right now. And if you are, let this be your encouragement: Delay is not denial. God's timetable is not your timetable, but His plan and timing are always intentional and for your good.

A Deeper Look at Jeremiah 29:11

We love to quote Jeremiah 29:11: "For I know the plans I have for you... plans to give you hope and a future." But do you know the context? That promise was spoken to a people who had just been exiled and were being told they would remain in that place **for seventy more years.** God's plan included waiting. But it also included hope.

Even when you feel stuck... God's not. He's still writing your story. Even when the current chapter feels like a painful pause, He's setting the stage for something redemptive and beautiful.

So don't confuse the silence with a lack of strategy. Sometimes, silence is preparation. Sometimes it's protection. But it's never punishment when you're walking with God. While you're waiting, ask God what you should do, and what you can enjoy each day, until His promise to you is fulfilled.

Final Encouragement

If your prayers feel unanswered, you are not alone. God's silence is not rejection. He is working in ways you cannot yet see. Keep praying. Keep trusting. Whether His answer is "Yes," "No," or "Wait," remember He is a good Father who always gives His best.

Let go of the timeline. Hold fast to His heart. Trust His Word and His character, and learn to wait well. Because when God finally answers, it's always worth it.

Prayer Journal Prompts:

- What is one prayer you've been waiting for God to answer? How has the waiting felt in your heart?
- What are three things God has done in past seasons that remind you He is faithful?
- If God never gave you what you're currently praying for, what would you still know to be true about His character?
- How can you make worship part of your waiting journey?
- What does Jeremiah 29:11 mean to you in this season?

Reflection Questions:

1. What emotions rise up in you when your prayers feel unanswered? Have you brought those honestly before God?
2. In what ways might God be protecting, preparing, or positioning you right now, even if you can't see it?
3. Who could you encourage or serve while you wait for your own breakthrough?
4. How can you begin to see this season of waiting not as wasted, but

as deeply sacred and purposeful?

Closing Prayer:

Father,

Waiting is hard. There are moments when I feel forgotten or discouraged, when it seems like You're not moving. But today, I choose to trust You. I believe You are a good Father, and even when the answers delay, I will cling to Your faithfulness. Strengthen my heart. Renew my hope. Let my waiting season become a season of worship. I surrender "the how", the timeline and rest in Your wisdom. You are always working for my good, even in the silence.

In Jesus' Name, Amen.

CHAPTER 10

Spiritual Warfare and Persistent Prayer

Praying Through the Battle, Becoming a Warrior in a Spiritual War

For we wrestle not against flesh and blood, but against principalities, against powers, against the rulers of the darkness of this world, against spiritual wickedness in high places. — Ephesians 6:12, KJV

It was just an ordinary Monday until it wasn't.

The day before, my teenage son limped into the house from the recreation center, clearly in distress as he had blown out his knee playing basketball. It was just days before Christmas, and like many families, we were already feeling the weight of holiday stress. My to-do list felt endless: meals to cook, laundry piling up, a house that needed tending, last-minute gifts to wrap, and a calendar packed with events and upcoming sports games. I was barely holding it all together. Then my husband walked through the door from work and quietly said, "I can't feel the right side of my body."

There was no time to process, no space to cry, and no room to fall apart. I didn't have the energy or capacity to *feel anything* about everything that was happening. I had to go straight into "this is an emergency" mode. My husband was having a stroke. I stayed calm, dialed 911, and did what I had to do to get him help. I held it together, barely, until the EMTs arrived and loaded him into the ambulance.

And then, as the flashing lights disappeared down the street, I crumbled. Crocodile tears spilled down my face, unstoppable. My body buckled under the weight of it all. But even in that moment, I knew I couldn't stay there. I still had to get up and pull myself together, to explain to my children what was happening, to ready our home and hearts for whatever came next, and somehow make my way to the hospital, all at once. The world didn't pause, even though *everything* in mine had shifted.

As if that moment wasn't heavy enough, I was also confronting something deeply personal and equally devastating: a painful betrayal by someone I had once trusted with my whole life was revealed. It was a moment in my life of complete unraveling.

That's when I realized, this wasn't just a series of unfortunate events. This was war. A full-blown spiritual attack targeting me, my family, our unity, our peace, and my faith. The enemy had launched an assault, and he wasn't playing fair. **But now...neither was I.** I chose to fight back, on my knees, with truth, with trusting in God's character, and in the power of prayer.

I stepped into what I can only describe as "Mama Bear Mode." But this time, I wasn't armed with to-do lists or raised voices. My weapons were spiritual. It was time to get quiet, be still and know (recognize, understand) that God is God (Psalm 46:10, AMP). On the way to the hospital and in the stillness between visits, I reached for my Bible. I filled the silence with sermons and whispered breath prayers when the words just wouldn't come.

Worship music became my refuge. I played it loud, so loud that fear, anger, and heartbreak had no space to linger. Whether in the house, in the car, or during my sanity-saving walks, I made a choice: to surrender and saturate my soul with God's presence. I surrounded my mind, body, and spirit with His Word and worship.

And slowly, something shifted. I remembered I wasn't alone. I wasn't powerless. God had already equipped me for this fight. No matter what lay ahead, one truth anchored me: **He would be with me every step of the way.**

As women and moms, we carry a unique calling, not only to nurture, guide, and protect, but to guard our homes spiritually. The battles we fight are often invisible, but their effects are very real. Ephesians 6:12 tells us we aren't wrestling against people, emotions, or circumstances; we're contending with spiritual forces that seek to unravel everything good God is building in our lives.

But here's the good news: we are not defenseless. We have God and the whole armor of God. We have authority in Jesus' Name. And we have the power of persistent prayer.

The Truth About Spiritual Warfare

Spiritual warfare isn't just for pastors, prophets, or seasoned intercessors; it's for you. It's for every believer who's ever felt life crashing down, who's ever fought for peace in the middle of chaos, or whispered a prayer through tears when words ran dry.

The enemy doesn't wait until we're strong. He doesn't ask permission. He strikes in the middle of our exhaustion, in the middle of our parenting, our marriages, our progress, our healing, our hope. He goes after what matters most, our peace, our unity, our joy, our trust in God. And more than anything, he wants to distort our view of our Heavenly Father. He wants us to believe that God has forgotten us, that prayer doesn't work, that maybe we're not even worth fighting for.

But let me remind you: **the devil is a liar** (John 8:44).

God has not left you defenseless. You are not alone in this. Jesus has already won the war. And because of that, you don't have to fight *for* victory. **You get to fight from victory, and that changes everything.**

You can pray with boldness, not just brokenness. You can stand with confidence, not just desperation. You are clothed in the full armor of God, and you've been given spiritual weapons *that work*. You are not meant to simply survive this season; you are equipped to overcome it.

So if you're in the middle of a battle right now, know this: God is still with you. He is still for you. He knows how to get you to victory and His good plans for your life. And He will carry you through, just like He did for me.

The Armor of God (Ephesians 6:10-18, AMP)

"In conclusion, be strong in the Lord [draw your strength from Him and be empowered through your union with Him] and in the power of His [boundless] might. Put on the full armor of God [for His precepts are like the splendid armor of a heavily-armed soldier], so that you may be able to [successfully] stand up against all the schemes and the strategies and the deceits of the devil. For our struggle is not against flesh and blood [contending only with physical opponents], but against the rulers, against the powers, against the world forces of this [present] darkness, against the spiritual forces of wickedness in the heavenly (supernatural) places.

Therefore, put on the complete armor of God, so that you will be able to [successfully] resist and stand your ground in the evil day [of danger], and having done everything [that the crisis demands], to stand firm [in your place, fully prepared, immovable, victorious]. So stand firm and hold your ground, having tightened **the wide band of truth** (personal integrity, moral courage) around your waist and having put on **the breastplate of righteousness** (an upright heart), and having strapped on your feet **the gospel of peace** in preparation [to face the enemy with firm-footed stability and the readiness produced by the good news].

Above all, lift up the [protective] **shield of faith** with which you can extinguish all the flaming arrows of the evil one. And take **the helmet of salvation**, and **the sword of the Spirit**, which is the Word of God." — Ephesians 6:10-18, AMP.

A Woman's Spiritual Strategy: The Armor of God

Here's what that looks like for a praying woman or mama:

1. **The Belt of Truth:** Start every day declaring what is true. "God is good. God is faithful. My family belongs to Him. His promises are still yes and amen."
2. **The Breastplate of Righteousness:** Live with integrity. Confess quickly. Apologize freely. Let your heart stay tender and aligned with God.
3. **Shoes of Peace:** Carry calm into chaos. Refuse to let tension define your tone. Walk into every room as a woman grounded in God's presence.
4. **The Shield of Faith:** Lift it up when doubt, fear, or lies start to come at you. Speak scriptures aloud. Proclaim, "My God is able."
5. **The Helmet of Salvation:** Protect your thoughts. When your mind whispers, "I'm not enough," respond, "I'm covered by grace."
6. **The Sword of the Spirit:** This is the Word of God. Speak it. Declare it. Believe it. Nothing cuts through darkness like scripture.

And then Paul adds this vital instruction: "Pray at all times, in every season, with all kinds of prayers" (Ephesians 6:18). That's our power source.

Don't Quit, Pray Without Ceasing

There will be moments when you feel like quitting, when your prayers feel dry, when the battles feel unrelenting, when heaven feels silent. But remember the persistent widow from Luke 18. She refused to give up. She kept showing up, knocking, believing. And Jesus said, if an unjust judge responded to that kind of persistence, how much more will your loving Father respond to you?

You're not begging a reluctant God; you're communing with a faithful Father.

- Keep praying, even when it feels like nothing is happening.
- Keep standing, even when your knees feel weak.
- Keep declaring, even when your voice trembles.

Because prayer is not about performance, it's about presence. It's about being aware of God's presence with you and refusing to let the enemy steal your voice, your hope, or your victory.

Spiritual Warfare in Real Life

I've walked through seasons where everything that could go wrong, did: illness, job loss, marital tension, parenting problems. My prayers felt like whispers into the wind. But I clung to God's Word as if it were oxygen. I wrote scriptures on sticky notes and index cards and placed them where I could see them every morning, reciting them while cleaning the house.

One day, a friend asked, "Why do you keep saying Bible verses out loud?" I told her, "Because the enemy can't read my mind, but he can hear me speak God's truth. And right now, we need truth to scream louder than the fear."

Things didn't change overnight. **But I did.** My faith got stronger. My spirit was steadier. And eventually, the breakthrough came on every front, one way or another.

In the early days after the trauma and emotional shock of what I had gone through, certain situations, words, or even tones of voice would instantly trigger me, like emotional landmines I didn't see coming. But over time, as I placed my emotions on God's altar and allowed Him to heal my heart layer by layer, those triggers began to lose their grip on me. What once sent me spiraling, now simply brushed against me, and I could breathe through it instead of breaking under it. Healing didn't erase the memory, but it strengthened my response. With prayer, support, and intentional soul work, I began to see progress. The emotional waves grew smaller, and my spirit grew steadier. That's the power of persistent prayer in spiritual warfare.

What to Do When You're Under Attack

1. **Worship Through It:** Turn up the praise. Sing until the lies lose their volume. Worship shifts atmospheres and puts the enemy on notice.
2. **Declare Truth:** Speak God's Word out loud over yourself and your family, over your mind, over your day.
3. **Pray with Others:** There's power in agreement. Text a trusted friend. Pray over the phone. You're not meant to fight alone.
4. **Cleanse the Atmosphere:** Pray through your home. Anoint the doorposts. Play worship music. Invite the Holy Spirit to saturate every room.
5. **Train Your Children (Proverbs 22:6):** Teach your children (your family, your community) to pray. To recognize spiritual attacks. To use scripture as their sword.

Spiritual Battle Plan Template

Here's a sample **weekly spiritual warfare rhythm** for your home:

Monday: Morning Armor Prayer (Ephesians 6:10–18)
Tuesday: Family Unity Focus (Pray against division)
Wednesday: Worship Wednesday Playlist
Thursday: Scripture Declaration Over Your Family Members
Friday: Gratitude Journal Entry and Testimony Time
Saturday: House Prayer Walk, Praying through your home
Sunday: Family Prayer and Communion

Final Encouragement

You are not powerless; you are a warrior daughter of the King. You were made for this. You were chosen for your family. You've been equipped with divine weapons and surrounded by God's presence. The battles may be intense, but the victory is already assured.

So pick up your spiritual sword, stand in your authority, and fight not in fear, but in faith. Your prayers are doing more than you can see. The enemy is trembling. Heaven is listening. And **God is moving.**

Prayer Journal Prompts:

- Where have I recently sensed spiritual resistance in my home or life?
- What scriptures bring me peace and strength in spiritual battle?
- How can I involve my children (or community) in prayer and worship this week?
- What spiritual "armor" do I need to put on more intentionally each day?
- How has God shown up for me in past spiritual battles?

Reflection Questions:

1. What area of your life feels under attack right now? Have you invited God into it fully?
2. How can you make prayer a consistent part of your daily battle strategy?
3. What lie has the enemy been whispering to you, and what is the truth of God's Word in response?
4. Who can you partner with in prayer this week?

Closing Prayer:

Heavenly Father,

Thank You for arming me with everything I need to stand firm in faith. Thank You for this next dimension of prayer that You have equipped me with. Thank You that I can pray offensively and not just defensively.

Thank You that I can shift atmospheres and environments with my prayers. When the battle feels overwhelming, remind me that You are my strength and my shield.

Help me to recognize the enemy's tactics and respond with truth, peace, and prayer. Help me to open spiritual doors that have been illegally closed, and shut doors that have been illegally opened.

Thank You that You have equipped me to commune with You and to protect my home, cover my children, transform my environment, and press forward with power. Thank You that I can contend with any force coming against me or my family.

Thank You that Your Word is true that when "the kingdom of heaven suffers violent assault, and violent men seize it by force [as a precious prize]" (Matthew 11:12, AMP). Thank You that "Yet in all these things we are more than conquerors and gain an overwhelming victory through Him who loved us [so much that He died for us]." (Romans 8:37, AMP).

Let me not grow weary in doing good. Train my mind and hands for war and my heart for worship. I declare that no weapon formed against me or my family shall prosper. I stand in victory, covered by Your love, clothed in Your righteousness, and led by Your Spirit.

In Jesus' mighty Name, amen.

Further Scripture Study on Spiritual Warfare:

If you ask Me anything in My name {as My representative}, I will do it. —John 14:14, AMP

Listen carefully: I have given you authority {that you now possess} to tread on serpents and scorpions, and {the ability to exercise authority} over all the power of the enemy (Satan); and nothing will {in any way} harm you. — Luke 10:19, AMP

And he spake a parable unto them to this end, that men ought always to pray, and not to faint — Luke 18:1, KJV

And let us not be weary in well doing: for in due season we shall reap, if we faint not. —Galatians 6:9, KJV

Fight the good fight of the faith {in the conflict with evil}; take hold of the eternal life to which you were called, and {for which} you made the good confession {of faith} in the presence of many witnesses. —1 Timothy 6:12, AMP

CHAPTER 11

Praying for Others

Becoming a Vessel of Intercession

Along my life journey, I've learned that prayer is one of the most powerful ways to love the people in our lives. Whether I'm praying for my children to make wise choices, for my husband to be healed and find strength in his daily work, or for a friend who is struggling, interceding for others isn't just a suggestion; it's part of our calling.

And he spake a parable unto them to this end, that men ought always to pray, and not to faint; — Luke 18:1, KJV

One of the greatest privileges we have as believers is the ability to lift others up in prayer. Intercession isn't just for pastors, prayer warriors, or leaders but for every believer with a heart willing to stand in the gap.

As women, mothers, sisters, daughters, and friends, we are uniquely positioned by God to recognize the emotional, spiritual, and practical needs of others and intercede on their behalf. This isn't just a personality trait or nurturing instinct; it's a divine assignment woven into our design.

Throughout Scripture, we see countless examples of women who noticed what others missed, responded with compassion, and became powerful vessels of prayer and advocacy.

From Esther, who risked her life to stand in the gap for her people (Esther 4:14-16), to Hannah, who poured out her soul in prayer not only for a child but also for the generations that would follow (1 Samuel 1:10-20), the Bible repeatedly affirms the spiritual sensitivity and prayerful boldness of women.

Mary, the mother of Jesus, discerned the moment for Christ's first miracle at the wedding in Cana (John 2:1-11), and the unnamed woman with the alabaster jar recognized the weight of Jesus' mission when others overlooked it, anointing Him in a prophetic act of worship and preparation (Luke 7:36-50, Matthew 26:6-13).

Jesus Himself consistently honored and responded to women who approached Him with faith and intercession, like the Syrophoenician mother who pleaded for her daughter's healing (Mark 7:24-30) or the Samaritan woman at the well, whose spiritual hunger led to the transformation of an entire village (John 4:1-42).

Why does this matter? Because intercession is often born from insight. And women, by God's grace, frequently carry a unique relational insight, discerning subtle emotional shifts, sensing spiritual tension in a home, or recognizing weariness in a friend's voice. We're often the first to feel when something's not right, and through prayer, we're called to bring it before the One who can make it right.

This sacred responsibility isn't just about empathy; it's about spiritual authority. James 5:16 reminds us that "the effectual fervent prayer of a righteous person avails much." That includes you. Your prayers, your petitions, and your Spirit-led instincts carry weight in the heavens. Whether you're whispering prayers over a sleeping child, crying out for a wayward loved one, or quietly standing in the gap for someone who doesn't even know you're praying, God hears. And God moves.

So pray boldly, consistently, and with confidence. You were made for this.

Shift Your Focus

There's something incredibly powerful about shifting your focus from your own needs to the needs of someone else. When we pray for others, we partner with Heaven in releasing breakthrough, healing, hope, and protection into their lives. And often, as we intercede for others, something shifts within us too: our perspective, our compassion, and our sense of purpose deepen.

I've had countless moments when God placed someone on my heart out of the blue: an old friend I hadn't spoken to in years, a struggling mom I saw at school pickup, or even a celebrity facing public scandal. Sometimes, I'll never know what my prayers did in those moments. But I do know this: every prayer matters. No act of intercession is wasted.

Intercession: The Heart of a Mother

If you're a mom, you probably already practice intercession more than you realize. Every whispered, "God, protect my babies," every time you sit in the school parking lot praying over your child's day, every nighttime prayer over a sleeping toddler, or texted prayer for your college-aged child. It's all intercession.

We are called to intercede for our families, our communities, our nation, and even our enemies. Jesus modeled this kind of prayer when He said from the cross, "Father, forgive them, for they do not know what they are doing" (Luke 23:34, NIV). And Romans 8:34 reminds us that Christ continues to intercede for us even now. When we intercede, we reflect the heart of Christ.

How to Pray for Others:

Be Sensitive to the Holy Spirit

Often, God will nudge your heart with a name or a burden. Don't ignore it. Take a moment to pray right then and there. Again, you don't have to have the perfect words, just a willing heart.

It's easy to pray for the people we love: our kids, our spouses, our friends (especially when they bring us that one gift, drink, or dessert to brighten our day). But Jesus calls us to a greater kind of love, one that stretches us beyond our comfort zone. Yep, that means praying for strangers… and even for that difficult coworker, the neighbor who never brings their trash cans in, and even for our enemies.

Jesus put it this way: "Love [that is, unselfishly seek the best or higher good for] your enemies and pray for those who persecute you." -Matthew 5:44 AMP.

God's heart is big enough for everyone, so let's widen our prayers to include:

- Those suffering around the world, because no one should feel forgotten.
- Church leaders and missionaries, because they're on the frontlines of faith.
- Our city and nation, because we all need wisdom, and our leaders do too.

- Schools, administrators, teachers, and students, because education shapes the next generation.
- Those facing injustice, because God is a God of righteousness and redemption.

Pray Specifically

Instead of just saying, "Lord, bless them," ask for specific things: peace, healing, provision, wisdom, protection, or clarity. If you know a child is struggling in school, pray for focus, confidence, and the right support. If a friend is walking through a divorce, pray for emotional strength, wise counsel, and God's comfort.

Prayer is most powerful when it's specific, kind of like when my kids ask for a snack. If they just say, "Mom, I'm hungry," I might hand them a banana. But if they say, "Mom, I want a peanut butter and jelly sandwich with the crusts cut off and a side of apple slices," well, now I know exactly what they're asking for!

God is a loving Father who delights in hearing our hearts. Instead of vague prayers like, "Lord, bless my family," take the time to tell Him exactly what's on your mind. "Lord, give my child wisdom in their friendships," or "Father, bring peace into my home today." The more specific your prayers, the more you'll recognize His specific answers, and that's where the real faith-building happens!

Pray Scripture

One of the most powerful ways to pray is by using God's own words, because His words are far better than ours (especially when we're running on an energy drink or coffee and three hours of sleep!).

A great way to do this is by inserting the person's name into Scripture as you pray. For example, instead of just saying, "Lord, bless my child," try praying, "Lord, I pray that [child's name] will trust in You with all their heart and lean not on their own understanding" (Proverbs 3:5-6).

Praying Scripture over others is like speaking heaven's language over your loved ones, declaring God's truth and promises directly into their lives. And the best part? God's Word never returns void (Isaiah 55:11), so you can pray with confidence, knowing He is working behind the scenes, even if that child you're praying for is currently throwing Legos at their sibling!

So will My word be which goes out of My mouth; It will not return to Me void (useless, without result), Without accomplishing what I desire, And without succeeding in the matter for which I sent it. — Isaiah 55:11, AMP

Therefore, pray in this way:

- "Lord, I pray that [Name] will trust in You with all their heart and lean not on their own understanding." -Proverbs 3:5-6
- "Father, fill [Name] with the knowledge of Your will through all spiritual wisdom and understanding." -Colossians 1:9

There's power in praying God's Word over your family and others. For example:

- For strength: "I pray that [Name] can do all things through Christ who strengthens her" (Philippians 4:13).
- For peace: "Let the peace of Christ rule in [Name]'s heart" (Colossians 3:15).
- For healing: "By His stripes, [Name] is healed" (Isaiah 53:5).
- For guidance: "Your word is a lamp to [Name]'s feet and a light to [Name]'s path." (Psalm 119:105).
- For protection: "The Lord is [Name]'s refuge and [Name]'s fortress, [Name]'s God, in whom [Name] trust." (Psalm 91:2).

Pray in Jesus' Name

As moms, we know what it's like to speak with authority, whether it's telling a toddler "No, you cannot wear your superhero cape in the bathtub" or reminding a teenager that curfew is not a suggestion. But did you know that you have even greater authority in Jesus' name? (John 14:13-14).

And I will do whatever you ask in My name {as My representative}, this I will do, so that the Father may be glorified and celebrated in the Son. If you ask Me anything in My name {as My representative}, I will do it. —John 14:13-14, AMP

When we pray for others, we're not just hoping things will change; we're calling on heaven's power to intervene! We're standing in the gap, declaring God's truth, and inviting His presence into situations that seem impossible.

So, whether you're praying over a child struggling in school, a friend facing hardship, or even that driver who just cut you off (yes, even them), remember this: your prayers carry weight, and when you pray in Jesus' name, heaven listens!

Be Persistent in Prayer

Some prayers take time. Kind of like waiting for a toddler to put on their own shoes or convincing a teenager to clean their room. It can feel like forever, but persistence pays off!

Remember, Jesus tells us in Luke 18:1-8 about a persistent widow who kept asking until she got justice. She didn't give up, and neither should we! Keep praying, even when you don't see immediate results, because God is always working, often behind the scenes in ways we can't even imagine.

When you feel like throwing in the towel, remember these scriptures and promises:

Pray without ceasing. —1 Thessalonians 5:17, KJV.

Yes, that means even when you're exhausted and running on caffeine and grace.

Let us not become weary in doing good, for at the proper time we will reap a harvest if we do not give up. —Galatians 6:9 NIV.

So, keep planting those prayer seeds, because one day, you'll see the beautiful harvest. Your prayers matter. Keep pressing in, keep believing, and keep trusting that God's timing is always perfect, even if it feels like He's taking a little longer than Amazon Prime!

Keep a Prayer List

Keep a running list of who you're praying for and what you're believing God to do in their lives. Update it as prayers are answered or needs change.

Follow Up: Let people know you're praying for them. Send a quick message or note. Ask how things are going. Intercession often opens the door for deeper relationships and spiritual conversations.

Praying for Difficult People

Some people are harder to pray for than others. Maybe it's someone who hurt you, betrayed you, or constantly pushes your buttons. But Jesus doesn't give us a pass here. Again, Matthew 5:44 tells us, "Love your enemies and pray for those who persecute you."

This doesn't mean we condone their behavior or pretend the pain didn't happen. It means we release them to God. We stop carrying the burden of bitterness and start asking God to do what only He can: change hearts, bring justice, and heal wounds. I can write this because I've had to live this. You, dear friend, are not alone.

Praying When Betrayal Breaks You

I know what betrayal feels like. The shock. The rage. The aching disbelief that someone you trusted, someone you may have loved or confided in, could hurt you so deeply. It's not just the act that breaks your heart; it's the shattering of what you believed to be true. It's the knowing that things will never be the same again.

When it happened to me, as it happens to so many, I wanted to pray like David did in the Psalms: *"Lord, smite them! Smite them and everyone who had a hand in this!"*

I was angry, wounded, and honestly, justified in feeling that way. Betrayal doesn't just bruise your feelings, it can traumatize your soul. It can make you question your worth, your discernment, and even your faith.

But the Holy Spirit didn't leave me in that place. Over time, **and it took time,** He began softening my heart. Gently. Patiently. He helped me shift my prayers. Instead of praying for revenge, I started praying for their healing. I prayed for the unhealed trauma, low self esteem, poor choices, insecurity, and spiritual disconnection that led to the condition of their heart...the condition that allowed betrayal to flow from it.

Did they change? Not right away. Maybe not at all in the beginning.

But I did. My peace returned. My clarity returned. And eventually, by the grace of God alone, the relationship started moving in a more positive direction. Not because I forced it, but because I had released it. I gave the entire situation and the traumatizing pain to God, and He began doing what only He can do.

Some wounds cut so deep, human words can't reach them and time alone won't heal them. But God can. Only He can touch the hidden places, mend what's shattered, and breathe life into what feels beyond repair.

If you're standing in the rubble of betrayal, heartbreak, or loss, I want you to hear this: God is still in the business of restoration. **What broke you does not have the final say.** He does.

Laying it all, every moment, every tear, every person involved, on the altar is not weakness. It's one of the most powerful, faith-filled acts of surrender you will ever make. Because when you release it into God's hands, you make room for Him to do what only He can: heal, redeem, and restore you fully. What they meant for evil God meant for your good. He will repay (see *Jeremiah 51:56, Ezekiel 11:21, Romans 12:19*).

As for you, you meant evil against me, but God meant it for good in order to bring about this present outcome, that many people would be kept alive {as they are this day}. —Genesis 50:20, AMP

...For the Lord is a God of {just} restitution; He will fully repay.
—Jeremiah 51:56, AMP

Beloved, never avenge yourselves, but leave the way open for God's wrath {and His judicial righteousness}; for it is written {in Scripture}, "Vengeance is Mine, I will repay," says the Lord. — Romans 12:19, AMP

Praying for Children at Every Stage

Toddlers:
- Safety and protection
- Peaceful sleep
- Teachable hearts
- Healthy development

Tweens/Teens:
- Wise friendships
- Identity in Christ
- Purity and discernment
- Protection from peer pressure and anxiety

Young Adults:
- Clarity in calling
- Godly relationships

- Financial wisdom
- Freedom from fear and comparison

Adults:
- Purpose and fulfillment
- Health and restoration
- Spiritual growth
- Relationships
- Business and career
- Marriage and parenting strength

30-Day Prayer List Template

Use this example format to intercede for someone different each day:

Day 1: Spouse
Day 2: Child #1
Day 3: Child #2
Day 4: Parent
Day 5: Sibling
Day 6: Close friend
Day 7: Pastor or spiritual mentor
Day 8: Church leadership
Day 9: Neighbor
Day 10: Community leader
Day 11: Teacher/educator
Day 12: Healthcare worker
Day 13: Essential worker
Day 14: Missionary
Day 15: Someone grieving
Day 16: Someone battling illness
Day 17: Someone unemployed
Day 18: Someone pregnant/new mom
Day 19: Someone struggling in faith
Day 20: A child in foster care
Day 21: Someone who hurt you
Day 22: A local business owner
Day 23: A school system or educator
Day 24: Someone who doesn't know Jesus
Day 25: Your city

Day 26: Your nation
Day 27: Another nation in crisis
Day 28: A random stranger you encountered
Day 29: Someone who inspired you
Day 30: Yourself

Reflection Questions:

1. Who in your life needs your intercession right now?
2. What specific promises from God's Word can you pray over them?
3. Is there anyone you've found difficult to pray for? What would it be like to surrender that person to God today?
4. How might your own heart be transformed through praying for others?

Closing Prayer:

Father,

Thank You for the gift and responsibility of prayer. Thank You for inviting me to partner with You in lifting others up. Teach me to be faithful in intercession, to be sensitive to Your Spirit, and to see people through Your eyes.

Help me pray not just when it's easy or convenient, but even when it costs me comfort or time. Let my heart break for what breaks Yours. And as I lift others before Your throne, I ask that You would transform my heart, too. Help me to release what has happened in our lives to You. Help me to pray daily for Your Kingdom to come and for Your will to be done in every situation. Make me a vessel of Your love, compassion, and truth.

In Jesus' Name, Amen.

CHAPTER 12
Leaving a Legacy of Prayer

Building Something Eternal

The call came at 2 AM.

My husband's voice carried a weight I immediately recognized. The kind of tone that tries to stay strong but trembles just beneath the surface. I could tell he was holding back tears.

"They're taking him into surgery," he said quietly. "The doctors said it's the only option. They have to proceed... please pray."

Our son had been taken to the hospital earlier that day, and I now had to be home with our other children. I was doing my best to try to steady my heart. In that moment, twenty-something years of motherhood narrowed into one crystal-clear realization: *I couldn't fix this.*

I couldn't rush to the hospital and make it better with my presence. I couldn't protect him from what was ahead. I couldn't offer advice or take away his pain. But I could pray. So I fell to my knees beside the bed, tears streaming, calling out to the same God who had carried this child (and all of us) through so many storms before.

Before I could even finish my first sentence, my husband added, "The anesthesiologist said, 'he prayed over him and God's got him.' And I feel at peace."

Those words sank into my soul like a balm. *God's got him.* That one sentence spoken by that anesthesiologist, a stranger, who may never fully understand the impact of his obedience and praying spirit, helped carry our entire family through the surgery that night.

When I shared the news with our other children, something beautiful happened; they began to pray too. Not because I told them to, but because prayer had already become a part of who they are.

In that sacred moment, I saw the fruit of every whispered prayer, every bedtime blessing, every faith-filled word spoken over them. This was the power of legacy. Prayer wasn't just something I did anymore, it had taken root in them. It had become their response too.

This is what it means to leave a legacy of prayer. It's not just about the moments we spend with God. It's about building a life that models intimacy with Him so clearly that others follow it, even after we're gone. It's a legacy that outlives us, echoing through generations.

The Eternal Investment

One generation shall praise Your works to another, and shall declare Your mighty and remarkable acts. — Psalm 145:4, AMP

Every prayer whispered in the stillness of night...

Every time we place a hand on our child's head and speak life into their future...

Every petition uttered for generations we may never meet...

These are not wasted words. They are eternal investments. Prayers don't disappear. They don't expire. They live on in the atmosphere we create around our homes, in the habits our children quietly observe, in the spiritual foundation we lay day by day. They take root in the unseen realm, where God is always at work.

I often think of my grandmother. She prayed over me, and every one of her grandchildren, before we were even born. She covered our lives in prayer as we grew, through every season, through storms we never told her about and decisions she never knew we made. And even though I didn't witness every prayer she prayed, I now know I have walked in the blessing of her intercession.

But there is one moment I'll never forget. I was with her (as I was with my own mother) as she transitioned into eternity. As her body grew weaker and her time on earth faded, something sacred and amazing happened.

She began to speak, not just to us, but to heaven. And what poured from her lips wasn't fear, or confusion, or last words of regret. It was scripture.

Bible verse after Bible verse flowed from her spirit as if heaven had been hidden inside her all along. She didn't just pray throughout her life, she became a prayer as she passed.

That moment marked me forever. I saw with my own eyes what a life of communion with God can look like when it's fully lived. I witnessed what it means to leave a prayer legacy so deep that even your final breath declares His Word. My grandmother didn't just invest in us, she invested in eternity.

And now I understand: this is what it means to leave a spiritual inheritance. It's not just about leaving something for your children, it's about leaving something in them.

Your prayers carry that same power. You may never see the full harvest with your own eyes, but rest assured, heaven never wastes a seed.

So pray with boldness. Live with unwavering faith. Worship with your whole heart. And trust that every spiritual investment you make, every whispered prayer, every tear-soaked plea, every moment of quiet obedience, is shaping generations you may never meet.

Just as my grandmother never knew this book would be written, you may never know the full reach of your faithfulness. But God knows. And in His hands, your legacy will go further than you could ever imagine.

The Three Pillars of a Prayer Legacy

Pillar 1: Model Prayer as a Way of Life

Prayer isn't just an event we attend or a one-time experience; it's a lifestyle we embody. It's not meant to be reserved for Sunday mornings, Wednesday evenings, or emergency moments. Prayer is the rhythm of a heart that stays connected to God in the everyday ordinary.

Our children or those we mentor don't just need us to teach about prayer; they need to witness it. They need to see that prayer isn't our last resort, but our first response. That it's not something we turn to only in crisis, but something that shapes our identity as believers.

Let them hear you pray over your home and marriage. Let them see you pause before responding to hard news or difficult behavior. Let them catch you praying while folding laundry, driving to work, prepping dinner, or walking the dog.

Normalize prayer. Not as a dramatic display, but as a natural, ongoing conversation with God. Let it be woven into your life so consistently that it doesn't feel like something you do, but simply who you are.

My kids used to laugh about how I'd pray over everything: lost items, lost socks, math tests, car keys, broken friendships, and broken hearts. But lately... I've heard them doing the same.

It stuck. And that's the goal, isn't it? Not perfection, not performance, but persistence. The kind of faith that quietly takes root in our homes and grows into habits our children will carry with them for a lifetime.

Because as funny as my prayers seemed to them, here's the truth: When we don't know where something is, God does. So why not ask?

Pillar 2: Create Prayer Traditions That Last

A praying home is a peaceful home. And the opposite is often true as well. When prayer is absent, confusion and disconnection quietly take its place. But here's the good news: you don't need to orchestrate elaborate devotionals or have perfect theology to build a spiritually rooted home. What truly lasts are the small, sustainable prayer habits that become woven into your family's daily life.

Traditions don't have to be complicated to be powerful. In fact, the simpler they are, the more likely they'll stick, and grow into something your children will carry with them into adulthood.

Start with what works in your current season. Maybe that's praying over your kids as you buckle them into their car seats or holding hands around the dinner table for a one-minute prayer of gratitude. Maybe it's a blessing whispered over them at bedtime or a Friday night "family prayer huddle" where everyone takes turns sharing what they'd like prayer for that week.

These moments, as ordinary as they may feel, are anything but. They become holy ground. They create a safe spiritual rhythm that teaches your family: This is what we do. This is who we are.

Daily Reminders

God told the Israelites to establish daily reminders of His Word so that it would become part of their lives and their children's memory: "These commandments that I give you today are to be on your hearts. Impress them on your children. Talk about them when you sit at home and when you walk along the road, when you lie down and when you get up" (Deuteronomy 6:6–7, NIV). He wasn't commanding grand gestures; He was inviting them into daily habits of faith.

That's what prayer traditions do. They normalize prayer. They remove the pressure of "doing it right" and instead focus on showing up together in God's presence.

Here are a few family-friendly prayer traditions to consider:

- **Morning Blessings:** Before leaving the house, speak a short prayer of protection and purpose over each child.
- **Mealtime Gratitude:** Go around the table and have each person thank God for one thing that day.
- **Scripture Sundays:** Choose a family Bible verse to pray and memorize together each week.
- **Prayer Walks:** Walk your neighborhood as a family and pray silently or aloud for neighbors, schools, and community leaders.
- **Holiday Intercession:** At Thanksgiving, Christmas, or birthdays, incorporate moments of prayer and praise specific to that season or individual.
- **Monthly Family Prayer Nights:** Light a candle, turn off the screens, and spend time praying together, no phones, just hearts.

These rituals become anchors in your family's spiritual life. And long after your children have grown and gone, they'll remember these moments. They'll find themselves doing the same with their own kids, praying familiar prayers in unfamiliar places, and remembering where they learned them first: in your home.

Let your house be the place where prayer isn't rare, it's routine. Let your living room become a sanctuary. Let your dining table echo with gratitude. Let your hallway be filled with blessings. That's the kind of tradition that builds legacies, and generations.

Find ways to implement:

- Morning declarations
- Bedtime blessings
- Mealtime blessings and gratitude prayers
- Sunday family prayer huddles
- Birthday, holiday, or milestone prayer circles

Keep **a family prayer journal** that tracks requests and testimonies. One day, your children and grandchildren will look through those pages and see the fingerprints of God.

Pillar 3: Teach Others to Pray

Teaching your children and family to pray is perhaps the most practical, powerful gift you can give. Start simple. Make it age-appropriate.

Toddlers (2–4):
- Thank-you prayers
- Praying over boo-boos

Children (5–10):
- Praying for others
- Learning the Lord's Prayer.

Let me pause here to thank my dad for taking the time to ensure we knew *the Lord's Prayer* when we were children. It will forever be in my heart and mind.

Tweens/Teens (11–18):
- Journaling their own prayers
- Praying for decisions and friendships
- Praying Scripture

Young Adults:
- Praying over their future
- Interceding for their generation
- Leading others in prayer

Train them to recognize the power and responsibility of spiritual leadership. Show them how to pray with boldness, with humility, and with expectation.

The Power of a Praying Family

A praying family is a strong family because life can get crazy. Between the early morning chaos of missing keys or shoes, homework crises, work deadlines, and last-minute snack requests, it's easy to rush through the day without pausing to pray.

But I've learned that when we make prayer a priority in our home, everything feels different, there's more peace, more unity, and more strength to handle whatever life throws our way. And trust me, on the days or seasons of life that we didn't pray together? Oh, I felt it.

So, let's be intentional:

- Pray over your children before they leave for school. Cover them in God's protection and wisdom (because let's face it, the world can be tough!).
- Pray with your spouse about decisions, challenges, and your future. Life is a team effort, and God is the best coach you could ask for.
- Pray for future generations. Ask God to bless and protect your family long after you're gone because your prayers don't expire.

As for me and my house, we will serve the Lord. —*Joshua 24:15, KJV*

This isn't just a lovely verse for a farmhouse sign; it's a declaration of who we are and what we stand for.

We're not always going to get everything right. Trust me, I know! And not getting things right can hurt really badly and cause damage. But here's the good news: as long as we have breath in our lungs, we have the opportunity to turn things around.

If prayer hasn't been a priority in your home, start today. Set this book aside for a moment, take a deep breath, and just talk to God. Invite Him into your life, your home, your relationships, and the situations that are causing you stress.

He's not distant. He's not waiting for you to have it all together. He is your Creator, and you can trust Him with your life and your journey. Take just one small step toward strengthening your relationship with Him today, and believe that you will see His goodness in your life. Because, friend, it's not over until it's over. So, keep believing. Keep praying, and watch how God moves in your family like never before!

I had fainted, unless I had believed to see the goodness of the Lord in the land of the living. — *Psalm 27:13, KJV*

Building Your Family Prayer Legacy

1. Write Your Family Prayer Vision

What do you want the spiritual climate of your home to look like? Write it down. Example: *"We will be a family who prays first, listens closely, and trusts God fully."*

2. Identify Your Non-Negotiables

Decide which practices you will commit to:

- ☐ Daily devotionals
- ☐ Bedtime prayers
- ☐ Weekly family intercession or evening prayer
- ☐ Weekly quiet time with God
- ☐ Verse of the Week: Pick one Bible verse to meditate on as a family
- ☐ Worship Night: Play worship music, sing together, or simply soak in God's presence with your family
- ☐ Serve Together: Volunteer monthly or weekly (even in small ways like writing cards to shut-ins or preparing a meal for someone in need).
- ☐ Gratitude Circle: Go around and share one thing you're grateful for each week. Do this at dinner or bedtime.
- ☐ Sunday Planning & Prayer: Before the new week begins, come together to pray over schedules, decisions, and challenges. Let God set the tone.

Let them become habits that shape your children's faith.

3. Document the Journey

Write prayers in journals, record video blessings, or save voice memos praying for your children's or grandchildren's future. These become spiritual time capsules that your family will treasure.

4. Train and Trust the Next Generation

Let them lead sometimes. Ask them to pray over you. Teach them to pray through Scripture. Encourage them to ask God big, bold questions. Show them how to pray when the answers take time.

The Compound Interest of Prayer: A God Who Multiplies

Prayer doesn't just add, it multiplies. And it doesn't just multiply over time; it multiplies through generations. That's because we serve a God of multiplication. From Genesis to Revelation, we see that what is placed in

God's hands never returns the same size; it returns bigger, fuller, richer, and more profound. That's true with fish and loaves. That's true with faith. And that's absolutely true with prayer.

One generation's whispered prayers become the foundation upon which another generation stands strong. One woman's or mother's whispered intercession can birth a movement of healing, purpose, and legacy.

Your quiet, unseen intercession, the kind you offer while folding laundry, weeping in the night, or pacing the floor in spiritual battle. Those are the seeds God multiplies into legacy, healing, and revival for those who come after you.

God is not merely in the business of addition; He specializes in exponential increase. He takes what we offer in obedience, no matter how small, and produces a harvest we couldn't produce on our own.

Let's look at a few scriptural examples that reveal this divine principle:

1. **The Widow of Zarephath** (1 Kings 17:8–16): She had just enough oil and flour for one last meal. But when she gave it to the prophet Elijah in obedience to God's instruction, that "last meal" turned into a supernatural supply that fed her family for many days. God multiplied her obedience.

2. **The Boy with the Loaves and Fish** (John 6:1–13): A nameless child offered his small lunch, five loaves and two fish, and placed it into the hands of Jesus. Jesus blessed it and broke the limits off of it. Not only was it enough to feed 5,000 men (plus women and children), but there were 12 baskets of leftovers. God multiplied what seemed insignificant into miraculous abundance.

3. **Abraham's Generational Blessing** (Genesis 22:17–18): When Abraham obeyed God in faith, even in the hardest command, God promised that Abraham's descendants would be "as numerous as the stars in the sky and the sand on the seashore." One man's obedience unleashed a covenantal blessing that would impact all nations through Jesus. God multiplied one man's obedience into a redemptive lineage.

4. **Hannah's Prayer for Samuel** (1 Samuel 1–2): She prayed in anguish for a child, and when God answered, she gave him back. That child, Samuel, became a mighty prophet and judge who would anoint Israel's first kings. Her single, tear-filled prayer changed the direction of a nation. God multiplied her faith into prophetic legacy.

And He's still doing it today.

So don't underestimate the impact of your prayers. You may think you're "just" praying over your child's attitude, or "just" asking God to heal a rift in your family. But in God's economy, your *"just"* is a seed, and every seed entrusted to God has the potential to grow into a harvest far beyond your lifetime.

Your consistent prayers, yes, even the tired, whispered ones, are forming spiritual momentum. They're pushing back darkness. They're planting roots in your children's hearts. They're watering promises yet to be fulfilled. And they're establishing a legacy that your grandchildren and great-grandchildren will walk in.

Prayer is generational stewardship. It is how we take what we've been given, faith, truth, and God's Word, and ensure it multiplies into the future.

This is what Jesus meant when He said, "This is to my Father's glory, that you bear much fruit, showing yourselves to be my disciples" (John 15:8, NIV). Bear fruit that remains, fruit that multiplies.

So yes, prayer is like compound interest. But even more so, prayer is like a mustard seed planted in faith (Matthew 13:31–32). Tiny at first, but when entrusted to God, it becomes a tree so large and full that others can find shade and shelter under it.

And that is the power of a praying woman. Especially one who keeps praying even when she doesn't see the harvest yet. Your consistent, everyday, even weary-sounding prayers are planting seeds. Those seeds will blossom into spiritual fruit that your great-grandchildren will benefit from. The ripple effect is real. So keep sowing, keep watering, and keep praying because the God of multiplication is at work in your legacy.

Legacy Action Steps This Week:

1. Write a letter or prayer to your future grandchildren
2. Start a family prayer tradition (such as bedtime, breakfast, or Sunday nights).
3. Record answered prayers in a visible place.
4. Speak a blessing prayer over each family member today.

Final Encouragement

The impact of your life, every moment, every prayer, every act of faith, matters. What you do today doesn't just affect you; it echoes into the lives of those who come after you. It will echo into eternity. Your prayers don't expire when you take your last breath. They continue to work, shape, and influence generations long after your journey here is complete.

Think about that for a moment. Every prayer you whisper over your children, every tearful petition for your family, every moment you spend interceding, it's a seed planted for tomorrow. Even if you don't see the fruit right away, trust that God is at work beneath the surface. Because He is.

You may not fully realize the fullness of your legacy during your lifetime. But one day, perhaps in heaven, you'll witness the generations changed by your prayers. The child you covered in intercession may go on to lead thousands to Christ. The family member you never gave up on may turn into the spiritual rock of their own home. The prayers you spoke over a future you'll never step into will still be working, echoing through eternity.

Don't underestimate the power of what you're building. The greatest legacy you could ever leave isn't in a trust fund or a title, it's in the trail of prayer behind you, paving the way for everyone who comes after.

Reflection Questions:

1. What kind of prayer legacy do I want to leave?
2. What are my family's current prayer habits, and how can I strengthen them?
3. Who can I begin training in prayer today?
4. How can I start documenting our family's spiritual journey?

Closing Prayer:

Father,

Thank You for the gift of legacy. Thank You for the reminder that my prayers are not wasted, they're seed sown into the soil of the future. Help me to be faithful in prayer, intentional in teaching, and bold in building a spiritual inheritance that will bless generations to come. May my home be a house of prayer, my children be warriors of faith, and my life a testimony of Your goodness. Let my words echo beyond my lifetime, and may every prayer leave a mark in heaven.

In Jesus' mighty Name, Amen.

Your legacy starts now. One prayer at a time.

Your Journey Is Just Beginning

Step Into Your Calling

You've made it to the end of this book, but truly, this is just the beginning of a beautiful, life-changing journey.

If there's one thing I pray stays with you long after you close these pages, it's this: **your prayers matter.** Your words carry power. Your voice reaches heaven. And your heart when turned toward God is a force that can shift atmospheres, restore hope, and spark revival.

Prayer is not just a backup plan for emergencies. It's not reserved for perfect women with polished words or uninterrupted mornings. (Spoiler: those don't exist!)

Prayer is your lifeline, your weapon, your peace, and your place of power. It's how you fight for your family, declare truth over your future, and walk confidently in the calling on your life, even when you're still figuring it out.

After they prayed, the place where they were meeting was shaken. And they were all filled with the Holy Spirit and spoke the word of God boldly. — *Acts 4:31, NIV*

That same power, that atmosphere-shaking, boldness-releasing, Spirit-filled power, is inside of you. Right now. Your prayers can shake rooms, shift circumstances, break generational curses, and release divine strategy and solutions. You're not just praying into the wind. You're partnering with heaven.

A Call to Deeper Intimacy

The greatest gift of prayer is not just the breakthrough, it's the relationship. Your Father isn't measuring your eloquence; He's leaning in to hear your voice. He longs for you to draw close, to whisper His name in the midst of your chaos, and to know that He's right there. Not judging. Not distant. Present.

Start simple. Start raw. Start where you are. "Hey, God..." is enough. Whisper His name when your house is noisy and your heart is overwhelmed. Cry out when you're at your limit. Thank Him when you see His hand. Invite Him into the ordinary. Because He meets us there, with peace, strength, wisdom, and just enough grace to take the next step.

Your Next Steps Into Power

Week 1: Lay the Foundation
- Choose a consistent daily prayer time.
- Create a quiet prayer space, even if it's just a corner of your kitchen.
- Begin with gratitude and declarations of who God is.
- Begin a prayer journal to record your requests and the answers you receive.

Week 2: Pray God's Word
- Choose five scriptures that align with your needs.
- Personalize and pray them daily.
- Speak them out loud to renew your mind.
- Write them on index cards or Post-its around your home.

Week 3: Expand Your Circle
- Intercede for friends, your church, your community, and your nation.
- Reach out to a prayer partner or join a prayer group.
- Lead your children or join your spouse in prayer once a week.

Week 4: Step Into Spiritual Authority
- Declare victory over the enemy's lies.
- Break strongholds in prayer using God's promises.
- Revisit and praise God for answered prayers.
- Begin mentoring someone else in prayer.

The Ripple Effect of Your Prayers

Your prayer life isn't just about you; it's about everyone connected to you. It's about your children, your spouse, your friends, and even strangers who will benefit from your intercession.

Every time you choose to pray instead of worry, heaven moves. Every time you speak God's Word over a situation, something shifts. Every time you show up in prayer, even when tired or discouraged, you're building a legacy that will outlast you.

The 90-Day Prayer Challenge

I challenge you to commit to 90 days of intentional, daily prayer. You don't need to be perfect, just be present. Set a timer. Write one sentence. Whisper one verse. Just start.

Days 1–30: Establish the habit

Days 31–60: Deepen intimacy and intercession

Days 61–90: Walk in authority and teach others

You will not be the same woman when you finish. You'll be stronger, more peaceful, and more confident in your God-given power.

If This Book Blessed You

Please don't keep it to yourself! You can:

- Gift a copy to a friend, sister, or daughter.
- Use it as a devotional in your women's group.
- Share your favorite quote online using #PowerfulPrayerLife
- Invite others to join you in the 90-Day Prayer Challenge.

Your voice and testimony matter. You never know who needs what you now carry.

A Final Word

As I write this conclusion, I'm praying for you. I'm praying that your confidence in prayer and in God will grow. That your intimacy with the Father will deepen. That you'll see breakthrough after breakthrough in your home, health, and heart. That you'll rise up and walk boldly as the faith-filled, prayer-powered woman you were always meant to be.

You are so deeply loved. Your prayers matter. And heaven is always listening. So go ahead. Raise your head. Lift your hands. Speak with boldness. Step into your next level. The world needs your powerful prayers, and for you to fulfill your purpose. Your journey starts now.

With all my heart and faith in you,
— *Marla*

P.S. I would love to hear how God is working in your life through prayer. Share your story with me on social media, or leave a review online. Your words may be the encouragement another woman is waiting to hear.

A Prayer of Salvation

If you've never asked Jesus into your heart, or if you've drifted and you're ready to come back home. I would like to personally invite you to join me in praying this simple yet life-changing prayer.

You don't have to have all the answers. You don't need to be perfect or have it all together. Just come with an open heart. God loves you deeply, and He's been waiting for this moment.

It would be my greatest joy to walk with you into the most important relationship you will ever have. Take a breath. Open your heart. Let's pray.

Heavenly Father,

Thank You for loving me, even when I didn't realize how much I needed You. Today, I acknowledge that I've tried to do life on my own, and I've fallen short. But I believe that You sent Your Son, Jesus, to die for my sins and rise again so that I could be forgiven, healed, and made whole.

Jesus, I invite You into my heart right now. Be my Lord, my Savior, and my forever friend.

Wash me clean. Make me new. Help me to live the life You created me for: full of love, purpose, joy, peace, and truth.

I surrender my past, my pain, my plans, and my pride. From this day forward, I choose to follow You. Lead, grow, and surround me with people who will walk this faith journey with me.

Thank You for saving me. Thank You for loving me. And thank You for never giving up on me. In Jesus' Name I pray, Amen.

Supporting Scriptures:

If you declare with your mouth, 'Jesus is Lord,' and believe in your heart that God raised him from the dead, you will be saved. —Romans 10:9, NIV

For God so loved the world that he gave his one and only Son, that whoever believes in him shall not perish but have eternal life. —John 3:16, NIV

Anyone who belongs to Christ has become a new person. The old life is gone; a new life has begun! — 2 Corinthians 5:17, NLT

For it is by grace you have been saved, through faith—and this is not from yourselves, it is the gift of God. —Ephesians 2:8, NIV

If you just prayed that prayer, welcome home, beautiful friend. Heaven is rejoicing, and so am I! You are fully known, fully loved, and finally found. Keep going. Keep growing. You are never alone again.

ABOUT THE AUTHOR

Marla A. McCarthy is the kind of woman you feel like you've known forever. She's the friend who prays for you when you can't find the words, the mom who gets what it means to pour from an empty cup, and the coach who helps you believe in yourself again.

As a wife of over 25 years, a mother of seven, and a certified Master Life and Empowerment Coach, Marla brings deep wisdom forged not just in classrooms but in the everyday moments of motherhood, marriage, and miracles. She's lived through the chaos, the burnout, betrayal, and breakthrough, and she's discovered that prayer isn't just something you add to your life. It anchors it. It's the power that holds everything together when life feels like it's falling apart.

Marla holds two degrees, one in Exercise Science Education from The Ohio State University and another in Healthcare Administration, along with multiple certifications in empowerment coaching, transformation, self-care, relationship coaching, and more. But her greatest strength isn't in her credentials. It's in her ability to connect women to the heart of God and to their own God-given potential.

As co-owner of The Real Life Series Publishing Company, Marla creates tools that help real women thrive in the real world. Through her books, signature coaching programs, retreats, and global online community, she has helped numerous women rediscover their true selves, reignite their faith, and reclaim the joy they thought they had lost.

She specializes in coaching women through:

- Faith-centered parenting and motherhood
- Mompreneurship and business growth without burnout
- Spiritual growth through prayer and biblical wisdom
- Emotional healing, confidence restoration, and self-care

Marla resides in Dallas/Fort Worth, Texas with her husband and their energetic crew of six sons and one daughter. If she's not coaching, writing, or speaking at an event, you'll likely find her cheering from the sidelines, cooking for a crowd, or sneaking in a moment of prayer in the midst of her beautifully busy life.

Her message is simple but life-changing: You don't need to be perfect to pray powerfully. You don't need to have it all figured out to walk in purpose. You just need a willing heart, a mustard seed of faith, and the courage to begin right where you are.

Marla believes deeply in the power of your voice, your story, and your prayers. She's honored to walk with you on this beautiful journey toward a more powerful, peace-filled, and purpose-driven life.

Let's stay connected!

Follow Marla @momlifewithmarla and visit marlamccarthy.com or momlifewithmarla.com for coaching resources, prayer journals, upcoming events, and new book releases.

Topical Scripture Index

About Prayer:
Deuteronomy 28:13
I Chronicles 4:10
Nehemiah 8:10b
Psalm 23:4
Psalm 37:4
Isaiah 53:5
Isaiah 54:17
Matthew 6:9-13
Mark 1:35
Mark 9:29
Mark 11:22-23
Luke 6:38
John 14:14
Romans 8:31
Philippians 4:13
II Timothy 1:7
Hebrews 11:1
I John 1:9
I John 4:4
1 John 5:14-15

Anger:
Psalm 37:8-9
Proverbs 14:16-17
Proverbs 14:29
Proverbs 15:1
Proverbs 16:32
Proverbs 25:21-22
Ecclesiastes 7:9
Matthew 5:22-24
Matthew 6:14
Romans 12:19
Ephesians 4:26
Ephesians 4:31-32
Colossians 3:8
Hebrews 10:30
James 1:19-20

Answered Prayer:
Psalm 37:4
Psalm 91:15
Psalm 145:18-19
Proverbs 15:29
Isaiah 65:24
Jeremiah 33:3
Matthew 6:6
Matthew 7:7-8
Matthew 18:19-20
Matthew 21:22
Mark 11:24
John 14:13
John 15:7
John 16:23
Hebrews 4:16
I John 3:22

Being a husband:
Proverbs 12:4
Proverbs 12:15
Proverbs 18:22
Proverbs 19:14
Proverbs 31:11
Proverbs 31:23
Proverbs 31:28
Ecclesiastes 9:9
Mark 10:12
Luke 16:18
Romans 7:2
1 Corinthians 7:2
1 Corinthians 7:3
1 Corinthians 7:4
1 Corinthians 7:9-11
1 Corinthians 7:14-16
Ephesians 5:23
Ephesians 5:25

Ephesians 5:33
Colossians 3:19
I Timothy 3:2
I Timothy 3:12
Titus 1:6
1 Peter 3:7

Being a wife:
Psalm 128:3
Proverbs 5:18-19
Proverbs 12:4
Proverbs 12:15
Proverbs 14:1
Proverbs 18:22
Proverbs 19:14
Proverbs 31:11
Proverbs 31:10-31
I Corinthians 7:3
Ephesians 5:21-33
Colossians 3:18
I Peter 3:1-7

Career & Business:
Deuteronomy 8:18
Deuteronomy 28:1-6, 8, 11-13
Joshua 1:8
I Kings 2:2-3
I Chronicles 22:13
Job 36:11
Psalm 1:1-3
Psalm 127:1
Proverbs 3:5-10
Proverbs 16:3
Proverbs 24:3-4
Isaiah 48:17
Matthew 6:33
Romans 12:11
Colossians 4:1
I Thessalonians

4:10-12
III John 1:2

Choices:
Deuteronomy 30:19
Psalm 1
Proverbs 3:5-6
Proverbs 4:20-22
Proverbs 12:15
Matthew 6:33
Matthew 16:25
Luke 10:41-42
John 10:27
Romans 8:6
Galatians 5:16
James 1:5

Confession:
Psalm 19:12-14
Psalm 25:7
Psalm 25:11
Psalm 25:18
Psalm 51:1-2
Psalm 51:10
Psalm 139:23-24
Isaiah 43:25
Mark 11:24
Romans 10:10
1 John 1:9

Confidence:
Proverbs 3:26
Isaiah 40:31
Isaiah 43:2
Habakkuk 3:19
Zechariah 4:6
John 14:12
Romans 8:37
II Corinthians 7:16

Ephesians 3:12
Philippians 1:6
Philippians 4:13
Hebrews 10:35-36
Hebrews 13:6
I John 3:21
I John 5:14-15

Confusion:
Psalm 32:8
Psalm 55:22
Psalm 119:165
Proverbs 3:5-6
Isaiah 30:21
Isaiah 40:29
Isaiah 43:2
Isaiah 50:7
I Corinthians 14:33
Philippians 4:6-7
II Timothy 1:7
James 1:5
James 3:16-18
I Peter 4:12-13

Courage:
Deuteronomy 33:27
Joshua 1:7
Joshua 1:9
Psalm 27:14
Psalm 31:24
Psalm 118:17
Isaiah 40:31
Isaiah 41:10
Isaiah 43:2
Isaiah 51:11
Romans 8:38-39
Philippians 4:6
Philippians 4:8
Philippians 4:13

I Timothy 5:14
I Peter 4:12-13

Depression:
Nehemiah 8:10
Psalm 30:5
Psalm 34:17
Psalm 147:3
Isaiah 40:31
Isaiah 41:10
Isaiah 43:2
Isaiah 51:11
Isaiah 61:1-3
Luke 18:1
Romans 8:38-39
II Corinthians 1:3-4
Philippians 4:8
I Peter 4:12-13
I Peter 5:6-7

Discouraged:
Psalm 27:1-14
Psalm 31:24
Psalm 138:7
Isaiah 51:11
John 14:1
John 14:27
II Corinthians 4:8-9
Galatians 6:9
Philippians 1:6
Philippians 4:6-8
Hebrews 10:35-36
I Peter 1:6-9

Divorce:
Deuteronomy 24:1-4
Proverbs 12:15
Jeremiah 3:1

Matthew 5:31-32
Matthew 19:3-9
Mark 10:2-12
Luke 16:18
I Corinthians 7:10-
17

Doubt:
Psalm 18:30
Isaiah 46:10-11
Isaiah 55:10-11
Isaiah 59:1
Mark 11:22-24
Luke 12:29-31
Romans 4:20-21
Romans 10:17
I Thessalonians 5:24
I Peter 4:12-13
II Peter 3:9

Effective Prayer:
Isaiah 1:15-16
Zechariah 7:8-13
Matthew 6:6
Matthew 14:23
Mark 1:35
2 Corinthians 7:14-
15
Ephesians 1:15-19
Colossians 4:2, 12
1 Thessalonians
5:17
James 5:16

Faith:
Matthew 9:20-22
Matthew 9:28-29
Matthew 17:20
Mark 9:23

Mark 11:22-24
Romans 1:17
Romans 10:17
Romans 12:3
II Corinthians 5:7
Hebrews 11:1
Hebrews 11:6
Hebrews 12:2
James 5:14-15
I Peter 1:7-9
I John 5:4

Family:
Exodus 20:12
Deuteronomy 6:6-9
Joshua 24:15
Psalm 127:3-5
Psalm 128:1-4
Proverbs 13:22
Proverbs 17:6
Proverbs 22:6
Proverbs 23:24
Proverbs 29:17
Isaiah 54:13
Malachi 4:6
Acts 16:31
Ephesians 4:31-32
Ephesians 5:21-6:4
Ephesians 6:4
I Timothy 3:4-5

Fear:
Psalm 23:4-5
Psalm 27:1, 3
Psalm 31:24
Psalm 56:11
Psalm 91:1
Psalm 91:4-7
Psalm 91:10-11

Proverbs 3:25-26
Isaiah 54:14
John 14:27
Romans 8:15
Romans 8:29, 31,
35-39
II Timothy 1:7
Hebrews 13:5-6
I John 4:18

**Financial
Problems:**
Deuteronomy 8:7-
14, 18
Deuteronomy 28:2-
8
Deuteronomy
28:11-13
Joshua 1:8
Psalm 23:1
Psalm 34:10
Psalm 37:25
Proverbs 13:22
Ecclesiastes 2:26
Malachi 3:10-12
Matthew 6:31-33
Matthew 10:8
Matthew 19:29
Luke 6:38
I Corinthians 16:2
II Corinthians 9:6-8
Philippians 4:19
III John 1:2

Forgiveness:
Isaiah 43:18-19
Matthew 5:10-12
Matthew 5:44
Matthew 6:14-15

Matthew 18:21-22
Mark 11:25
Luke 17:3
Romans 12:21
Ephesians 4:31-32
Philippians 3:13-14
Colossians 3:13
Hebrews 10:30
I Peter 2:19-23
I Peter 3:9-10
I Peter 4:12-14

God's faithfulness:
Genesis 9:16
Genesis 28:15
Deuteronomy 7:8-9
Joshua 23:14
I Kings 8:56
Psalm 36:5
Psalm 40:10
Psalm 89:1
Psalm 89:2
Psalm 89:5
Psalm 89:8
Psalm 89:33-34
Psalm 92:2
Psalm 119:65
Psalm 119:90
Psalm 121:3-4
Psalm 143:1
Isaiah 25:1
Isaiah 54:9-10
Lamentations 3:23
1 Corinthians 1:9
I Corinthians 10:13
I Thessalonians 5:24
II Thessalonians 3:3
II Timothy 2:13, 19
Hebrews 10:23

I Peter 4:19
II Peter 3:9
I John 1:9

God's Guidance:
Joshua 1:8
Psalm 16:11
Psalm 18:30
Psalm 19:7
Psalm 19:9-11
Psalm 23:3
Psalm 32:8
Psalm 37:23
Psalm 119:9-11
Psalm 119:24
Psalm 119:105
Proverbs 6:22-23
Proverbs 16:25
Isaiah 2:3
Isaiah 30:21
Luke 1: 70, 79
John 8:31-32
John 10:3
II Timothy 3:16-17
II Peter 1:4

God's Will:
Exodus 33:13
Joshua 1:8
Nehemiah 9:20
Psalm 17:5
Psalm 25:4-5
Psalm 31:3
Psalm 32:8
Psalm 37:23-24
Psalm 43:3
Psalm 48:14
Psalm 119:105
Psalm 119:133

Psalm 143:8
Psalm 143:10
Proverbs 3:5-6
Proverbs 6:22-23
Proverbs 16:3
Isaiah 30:21
Isaiah 48:17
Isaiah 58:11
John 16:13
James 1:5

Grief:
Psalm 23:4
Psalm 119:50
Isaiah 41:10
Isaiah 43:2
Isaiah 49:13
Isaiah 51:11
Isaiah 61:1-3
Jeremiah 33:3
Matthew 5:4
I Corinthians 15:55-57
II Corinthians 1:3-4
II Corinthians 5:8
I Thessalonians 4:13-14
II Thessalonians 2:16-17
Hebrews 4:15-16
I Peter 5:7
Revelation 21:4

Health & Healing:
Exodus 15:26
Psalm 103:3
Psalm 107:20
Proverbs 4:20-22
Isaiah 53:5

Jeremiah 17:14
Jeremiah 30:17
Matthew 8:8
Matthew 9:35
Mark 16:17-18
Luke 6:19
John 6:63
Hebrews 13:8
James 5:14-15
I Peter 2:24
III John 1:2

Joy:
Nehemiah 8:10
Psalm 16:11
Psalm 30:5
Psalm 105:43
Psalm 126:5
Ecclesiastes 2:26
Isaiah 51:11
Habakkuk 3:18
John 15:10-12
John 16:20
John 16:24
Acts 2:28
Romans 5:11
Romans 14:17
Romans 15:13
Galatians 5:22
Philippians 4:4
Jude 1:24

Loneliness:
Deuteronomy 4:31
Deuteronomy 31:6
Deuteronomy 33:27
I Samuel 12:22
Psalm 27:10
Psalm 46:1

Psalm 147:3
Isaiah 41:10
Isaiah 54:10
Matthew 28:20
John 14:1
John 14:18
Romans 8:35-39
Hebrews 13:5
I Peter 5:7

Love:
Jeremiah 31:3
Mark 12:30-31, 33
John 3:16
John 13:34-35
John 14:21
John 15:9-10
John 15:12-14, 17
John 16:27
Romans 5:8
Romans 8:38-39
I Corinthians 13:1-
    8, 13
I John 4:7-8
I John 4:10-12
I John 4:16, 21

Marriage:
Genesis 2:18
Genesis 2:24
Proverbs 3:5-6
Proverbs 18:22
Jeremiah 29:6
Hosea 2:19, 20
I Corinthians 7:2-4
Ephesians 5:22-33
I Timothy 5:14
Hebrews 13:4
I Peter 3:1

I Peter 3:7

Marital Problems:
Genesis 2:18
Genesis 2:24
Joshua 24:15
Psalm 101:2
Psalm 119:1-2
Proverbs 3:5-6
Proverbs 10:12
Romans 13:10
Ephesians 4:31-32
Ephesians 5:21-33
I Peter 1:22
I Peter 3:1-7
I Peter 3:8-11

Patience:
Psalm 27:14
Psalm 37:7
Psalm 37:8-9
Psalm 40:1
Ecclesiastes 7:8-9
Isaiah 40:31
Lamentations 3:26
Romans 5:3-5
Romans 8:25
Romans 15:4-5
Galatians 5:22
Hebrews 6:12
Hebrews 10:35-37
Hebrews 12:1
James 1:3-4
James 5:7-8

Peace:
Psalm 37:11
Psalm 37:37
Psalm 119:165

Proverbs 17:14
Isaiah 26:3
Isaiah 26:12
Isaiah 55:12
Isaiah 57:2
John 14:27
Romans 5:1
Romans 8:6
Romans 12:18
Romans 14:17-19
Romans 15:13
II Corinthians 13:11
Philippians 4:6-7
Colossians 3:15
James 3:16

Pleasing God:
II Chronicles 5:13, 14
Psalm 47:1
Psalm 109:30
Psalm 145:21
Psalm 147:11
Psalm 149:1-6
Isaiah 43:7, 21
John 4:23, 24
Romans 8:8-9
Romans 12:1-2
Colossians 1:10
I Timothy 2: 1, 3, 8
Hebrews 11:6
Hebrews 13: 15-16
I Peter 2:5, 9
I John 3:22
Revelation 4:11

Prayer for Others:
Deuteronomy 9:26
1 Samuel 1:27

1 Kings 8:48-50
2 Chronicles 7:14
Ezra 6:10
Nehemiah 1:11
II Corinthians 13:14
Philippians 1:9-11
Colossians 1:9-11
I Thessalonians 5:23
II Thessalonians 2:16-17
II Thessalonians 3:5
Hebrews 13:20-21

Prosperity:
Deuteronomy 8:18
Deuteronomy 26:1-2
Deuteronomy 28:2
Joshua 1:7
Psalm 35:27
Psalm 112:1, 3
Proverbs 1:32
Proverbs 3:9-10
Proverbs 13:21
Proverbs 22:7
Malachi 3:10-12
Luke 6:38
2 Corinthians 9:7-8
Galatians 3:29
Galatians 6:7
Ephesians 4:28
Philippians 4:19
I Timothy 6:17
III John 1:2

Protection:
Psalm 91

Salvation:

Matthew 10:32
John 1:12
John 3:16
John 3:17
John 3:36
Romans 3:23
Romans 5:8
Romans 5:12
Romans 6:23
Romans 10:8-10
1 Corinthians 15:1-4
Ephesians 2:8-9
I John 5:11-13
Revelation 3:20

Single Life:
Psalm 37:4
Proverbs 3:5-6
Proverbs 12:15
Hosea 2:19
Romans 7:4
1 Corinthians 6:13
1 Corinthians 6:18
I Corinthians 7:8-9
I Corinthians 7:27-28
I Corinthians 7: 32-33, 35
I Corinthians 7:37
Galatians 6:4
Hebrews 13:4
II Peter 1:6-8

Spiritual Growth:
Psalm 92:12
II Corinthians 3:18
Ephesians 3:14-19
Ephesians 4:14-15

Philippians 1:6,
9-10
Colossians 1:9-11
Colossians 3:16
I Timothy 4:15
II Timothy 2:15
Hebrews 6:1
I Peter 2:2-3
II Peter 1:5-8
II Peter 3:18

Temptation:
Psalm 119:11
Proverbs 28:13
Romans 6:14
I Corinthians 10:12-
13
Ephesians 6:10-11,
16
Hebrews 2:18
Hebrews 4:14-16
James 1:2-3, 12
James 1:13-14
James 4:7
I Peter 1:6-7
I Peter 5:8-9
II Peter 2:9
I John 1:9
I John 4:4
Jude 24-25

Trials & Troubles:
Psalm 31:7
Psalm 121:1-2
Psalm 138:7
Isaiah 43:2
Isaiah 51:11
Nahum 1:7
Matthew 6:34

John 14:1
John 16:33
Romans 8:28
II Corinthians 1:3-4
II Corinthians 4:8-9
Philippians 4:6-7
Hebrews 4:15-16
I Peter 5:7

Unsatisfied:
Psalm 34:10
Psalm 37:3
Psalm 63:1-5
Psalm 103:1-5
Psalm 107:9
Proverbs 12:14
Isaiah 1:19
Isaiah 12:2-3
Isaiah 44:3
Isaiah 55:1
Jeremiah 31:14
Joel 2:26
Matthew 5:6
Matthew 6:33
II Corinthians 9:8
Philippians 4:12-13

**Unsaved Loved
Ones:**
Genesis 22:18
Psalm 55:22
Psalm 98:2
Proverbs 22:6
Isaiah 44:3
Isaiah 50:10
Isaiah 56:1
Matthew 18:14
John 16:7-8
Acts 11:14

Acts 16:31
I Corinthians 7:13-
16
I Thessalonians
5:21-22
I Thessalonians 5:24
I Peter 3:1-2
II Peter 3:9

Victory:
Psalm 33:10
Isaiah 1:19
Isaiah 54:17
Matthew 7:7
Mark 11:24
John 1:4-5
John 16:33
Romans 8:37
I Corinthians 15:57
II Corinthians 2:14
II Corinthians 4:17
Ephesians 6:13-17
Philippians 4:13
I Thessalonians 5:18
II Timothy 2:3
I Peter 5:9-10
I John 2:14
I John 4:4
I John 5:4
I John 5:5

Waiting:
Psalm 27:14
Psalm 33:20
Psalm 62:5
Psalm 130:5
Psalm 145:15-16
Isaiah 25:9
Isaiah 40:31

Habakkuk 2:3
Hebrews 10:23
Hebrews 3:14

Widows:
Deuteronomy 10:18
Deuteronomy 27:19
Job 29:13
Psalm 68:5
Psalms 146:9
Psalm 147:3
Proverbs 15:25
Isaiah 54:5
Jeremiah 49:11
Matthew 28:20
John 14:18
John 16:22
I Corinthians 7:39-
        40
Philippians 4:19
Hebrews 13:15
James 1:27

Wisdom:
Job 12:13
Proverbs 1:7
Proverbs 2:6-7
Proverbs 3:13
Proverbs 4:7-9
Proverbs 5:1
Proverbs 8:11
I Corinthians 3:19
James 1:5, 3:16-18

Worry:
Psalm 4:8
Psalm 91:1-2
Psalm 119:165
Proverbs 3:24

Isaiah 26:3
Matthew 6:25-34
John 14:1
John 14:27
Romans 8:6
II Corinthians 2:14
Philippians 4:6-7
Philippians 4:19
Colossians 3:15
Hebrews 4:3, 9
I Peter 5:6-7

ALSO AVAILABLE FROM
THE REAL LIFE SERIES PUBLISHING CO.

Enhancing Your Journey:
90-Day Prayer Journal
by Marla A. McCarthy
ASIN: B0F37TRD72
Available at Amazon.com

Create The Life You Want:
Your 90-Day Roadmap to Purpose, Balance, and Success
by Marla A. McCarthy
ISBN: 979-8-9989754-2-4

Create The Life You Want:
90-Day Goal Journal
by Marla A. McCarthy
ASIN: B0F4W9YRP7
Available at Amazon.com

The Ten Commandments of Friendship:
Sisterhood Principles Every Woman Should Live By
by Marla A. McCarthy
ISBN: 979-8-9989754-4-8

Loving Me:
A Guide To Renewing Your Mind, Body & Spirit
by Marla A. McCarthy
ISBN: 979-8-9989754-5-5

Be a Seed:
Grow Deep. Rise Strong. Multiply Good
by Marla A. McCarthy
ISBN: 979-8-9989754-6-2

www.ingramcontent.com/pod-product-compliance
Lightning Source LLC
Chambersburg PA
CBHW031421120626
46545CB00006B/2216